Hot Brass Tacks
Can a Dozen Statements Change Your World?

From the dictionary ...
hot *adj Informal*
Most recent; new or fresh: *a hot news item; the hot fashions for fall.*
Currently very popular or successful: *one of the hottest young talents around.*
Requiring immediate action or attention: *a hot opportunity.*

brass tacks *pl. n. Informal*
Essential facts; basics: *getting down to brass tacks.*

From the thesaurus ...
brass tacks *Definition:* the facts *Synonyms:* basic facts, basics, cases, essential facts, essentials, facts, nitty-gritty, realities, the dope, the scoop, the whole story, truth of the matter

Copyright © 2005, 2009 by Kainos Enterprises

All rights reserved. No part of this book may be reproduced in any form or by any electronic or mechanical means, including information storage and retrieval systems, without permission in writing from the publisher, except by a reviewer who may quote brief passages in a review.

Published By: Kainos Enterprises
                7777 Churchville Road
                Brampton Ontario Canada L6Y 0H3
                905-230-8116

ISBN: 0 - 9685427 - 2 - 7

All scripture quotations, unless otherwise indicated, are taken from the HOLY BIBLE, NEW INTERNATIONAL VERSION®. NIV®. Copyright ©1973, 1978, 1984 by International Bible Society. Used by permission of Zondervan. All rights reserved.

Contents

See Ball. Hit Ball. 5
I Never Said That! 11
    "I tell you the truth ..."
It's Time! 17
    "The time has come."
Moving Targets 25
    "The people were amazed at his teaching, because he taught them
    as one who had authority, not as the teachers of the law."
Good Government 33
    "The kingdom of God is near."
Twin Essentials 39
    "Repent and believe the Good News!"
Go Fishing 47
    "Come, follow me and I will make you fishers of men."
Needy People 57
    "It is not the healthy who need a doctor, but the sick.
    I have not come to call the righteous, but sinners."
It's a Secret! 63
    "He who has ears to hear, let him hear."
Story Telling 69
    "This is what the kingdom of God is like."
First Presentation 79
    "Take nothing for your journey except..."
Matters of the Heart 85
    "...it is what comes out of a man that makes him 'unclean.'"
What's His Name 91
    "Who do people say I am?"
The Price and The Prize 99
    "If anyone would come after me, he must deny himself and take
    up his cross and follow me."
Kid's Stuff 107
    "I tell you the truth, anyone who will not receive the kingdom of
    God like a little child will never enter it."
Sad Stories 115
    "Why do you call me good? No one is good—except God alone."
The Rules 123
    "You are not far from the kingdom of God."
Bible Reference Index 130

"Everything should be made as simple as possible but not simpler."

Albert Einstein

1

See Ball. Hit Ball.

He was known as "Charlie Hustle." Forgive me if you are not a baseball fan; I will explain in a moment. But if you are a baseball fan you probably know who I am referring to. He once said, "I'd walk through hell in a gasoline suit to keep playing baseball." He was not good at a lot of things. His ex-wife once said, "It was too bad I wasn't a second baseman; then I'd probably have seen a lot more of my husband." One of his baseball buddies said, "_____ is the most likeable arrogant person I've ever met." He isn't in the Hall of Fame. Ask any true baseball fan, "Why not?" and he/she will give you the answer with a look that says, "Doesn't everybody know that answer already?"

He was good at one thing. Hitting. Again for the non-baseball fan, that is the part of the game where you stand in a predefined place beside a seventeen inch wide white thing. (It is made of rubber and I have no idea why they call it "the plate." You can just accept that.) A guy on a twelve inch hill puts his foot on the front edge of another white thing. (This one is also made of rubber but this time they call it "the rubber." Don't try and figure that out. You may get a headache. Just work with me here.) "The rubber" is precisely 60 feet 6 inches away from the first white thing. That guy, appropriately called "the pitcher" throws a little white hard ball in as deceptive a way as he can, so that you can't take a swipe at it with a finely and precisely shaped piece of hickory wood and get the ball to go where you want it to go. That's hitting. They pay grown men thousands of dollars each time they stand there and try to do that. They only have to succeed between 2.5 and 3 times out of 10 to get paid outrageous dollars to try.

They say that is the hardest thing in sports to do well. They talk about the "mechanics." They study videos of others doing it. They study videos of themselves both succeeding and failing at it. They talk about "stance", "grip" and "head movement." Then they get technical — "opening up too early", "an inside out swing", "pull hitting" and "out in front." It gets complicated. In fact, when they use the term "seeing the ball," they don't mean just "seeing the ball"; they mean actually seeing the precise velocity, direction and rotation on the ball at the moment the ball leaves the pitcher's hand so that they can get the bat started in the right direction at the right time. Apparently, "seeing the ball" isn't easy. It is a skill that fades in and out for even the best of hitters. When they are in the "zone" as they say, they say they are "seeing the ball" better. The rest of us don't really understand. We have a hard enough time following that silly little white thing after we do hear the crack of the bat meeting the ball. And, by the way, on a day at the ballpark when you hear that crack, it creates a noisy and exciting event. It doesn't happen all that often.

Charlie Hustle was different. Oh he had his ups and downs in his chosen pursuit. But he did it better than anybody. In fact, he said it all came down to this for him, "See ball. Hit ball." Yogi Berra, another great ball player, is more famous for his quotes. He once said, "You can't think and hit at the same time." That is sort of the same but Charlie Hustle made it even simpler and he did it better than Yogi anyway. "See ball. Hit ball."

What has this got to do with anything? Not much. I just like telling the story. The baseball fans get it as if there is some cosmically profound truth shrouded here. Actually, I have to admit it, I think Charlie Hustle was on to something. If I have the facts right he just didn't apply it well to much other than baseball. I don't know if he has figured it out since he retired.

I want us to take a "See ball. Hit ball." approach to the words of Jesus. I don't want to make this complicated. It isn't complicated. In fact, if we don't start with the plain and obvious meaning of the words of the Master we will end up perplexed and confused. When it comes to life we won't do nearly as well as we could. Keep it straightforward. Start with the basics. Don't go getting fancy.

This book is for anyone who wants to cut through to the essentials when it comes to the words of Jesus. I have found a steady stream of people throughout life who are confused about what Jesus said, who he was and how he related to people. There are three groups to consider. The first is folks who have never attended any form of meeting of Jesus' followers. The second is those who have attended and sometimes they have attended regularly all their life. The third group is made up of those who have dropped out for one reason or another. Often they have become disillusioned by the behavior of some individual or group. People in all three groups are confused about what Jesus actually said and how he behaved. There are different kinds of confusion. From time to time you will hear people via the media say things such as, "Jesus would never say that." I wonder how they formed that opinion. Often I could take them to actual recorded words from Jesus that would point to the possibility that their blanket affirmation is very debatable. We won't be covering everything Jesus put on the record. But at the same time we won't be just pulling out random statements out of context to make him fit a particular image.

Within an hour I predict that with this "See ball. Hit ball." approach you are going to hear some shocking things out of the mouth of Jesus. You might even get angry and say, "Why hasn't anyone ever pointed that out to me before?" I predict that you will have some strong feelings. If you are tempted to discount the way I explain the message I hope you will hear me out and make sure that you bring actual facts to back up your resistance and not just things you presume to be true. Make sure you have the facts as your foundation. When you get down to it there may have been a lot out there that kept these facts hidden from you until now. You will have to decide what you think of these statements for yourself. But at least, I request you give Jesus the respect to make an honest effort to hear what he intended people to hear. Once you know the raw facts then you can take it forward to the next level if you choose.

Later there might just be more that needs to be added to round out the picture. There is always the need to balance truths with one another. Concepts that are in harmony sometimes have offsetting virtues and merits that temper our understanding. But I am not going there very often in this book. The libraries are full of that sort of material. I want to just get back to basics. See ball. Hit ball. There are other ways to engage your interest. We could start from psychology or sociology to point out the benefits of following Jesus. There is a solid body of evidence to consider from various research studies. We are simply not going there today. Maybe some other time. We are sticking to the high impact statements of Jesus. These statements are like hot brass tacks.

In baseball, all the eyes are on the pitcher and batter. The batter only gets the spotlight in sequence one out of 8 or 9 times his team is at bat. A good pitcher may have about 100 times to throw the ball in a given game. But the batter only gets between 3 and 5 times to actually get his chance to hit that ball. He gets three strikes each time and then he is out if he can't make it happen. He only has to succeed much less than half the time to win the home crowd's favor. He had better understand the basics. See ball. Hit ball. The pitcher's agenda is to deceive the batter with various amazing techniques—all within the rules. Advantage pitcher. Even bad ones get more "outs" than batters get "hits." It may be the hardest thing to do in sports. But it obviously can be done. See ball. Hit ball.

You know this isn't a book about baseball. But it is a book about touching on the essential details. It is about hot brass tacks. The issues we are about to face are of ultimate importance. Are you ready to take it straight up? Let me warn you, if you are ready with a "See ball. Hit ball" attitude you are going to understand things that will challenge you. They will challenge what your parents taught you. They will challenge what the media teaches you. They will challenge what your spiritual leader taught you (errr, unless it was me, of course *GRIN*). They will challenge what your professor taught you—even your religious studies prof. These words will challenge you at the deepest level of your personality if you will let them. The words have been around for nearly

2000 years but you haven't. So for you there is only one short lifespan to respond.

Are you open to adjusting your thinking? Look. Even if you don't choose to change what you believe, at least, are you ready to be intellectually honest with what Jesus said? If you are going to reject his teaching you at least want to be sure you aren't just rejecting a pale imitation.

You won't be offended at me if I tell you the truth, will you? You do promise me that you will go back to the original documents (Matthew, Mark, Luke or John) and verify that what I say he said and meant is what he actually said and meant, won't you? I will explain a little about these documents in chapter three. But I do want you to consider the meaning in those original words as of prime importance. I really have no interest in getting you to believe me or as you might put it "your version of the truth." I don't mind if you go and get a second opinion or form your own.

I hope you will put the searchlight of Jesus' words straight on all opinions. This is all about your personal pursuit of knowing the truth. You have to battle your way through all this for your own sake. Oh sure, you can walk away because it is too challenging. Frankly, most people do. This isn't a popularity contest. You don't get to punch numbers into your cell phone and vote the winner.

You are welcome to communicate with me directly. I will pay close attention to what you say. I will make an honest attempt to correct my thinking and my way of communicating if I see your point. But if you disagree with Jesus you had better take that up with him.

So here we go. See ball. Hit ball. And by the way Charlie Hustle's real name is Pete Rose. But all the baseball fans already knew that.

For us, "See ball. Hit ball" is about the direct meaning in the words of Jesus. Now, let's learn what he said. Or to mix our metaphors, let's get down to some hot brass tacks.

"I tell you the truth ..."

*Jesus
quoted 13 times in Mark*

2

I Never Said That!

It happens in the school yard, the legislature, the office or plant and in the kitchen. It causes hurt and indignation. The natural inclination is to respond with our primal fight mechanism. It has happened to you and me. In fact, it is a very common human experience and none of us like it.

"I never said that!" "That's not what I meant and you know it." Hands on hips. Furrowed brow. Strident tone. Somebody has twisted somebody else's words or at the minimum the meaning behind the words that were used. Bong! Round one.

You are, no doubt, aware that the tone by which something is said impacts its meaning. But somehow normally we are able to muddle through all that and catch the meaning the other person intends. However, sometimes it is more useful for argument's sake to play dumb. It is more useful to ignore the point by reducing it to the absurd. Now certainly there is plenty of room for simple misunderstandings. Those frustrate us but can be soothed away by more conversation. I'm not referring to that kind of misrepresentation or simple misunderstanding.

I'm referring to the situation in which somebody makes a point, the meaning of which is clear, and somebody else deliberately twists its meaning. Normally it happens because they don't like what is being said. They want to twist the words or put them in another context or tone to their own advantage. That is when our blood boils. This situation is exacerbated when a third party takes up this misrepresentation and innocently portrays the misrepresented view as the original meaning.

For many years I have wondered how Jesus takes it when we misquote him and misrepresent him. I don't think that it is difficult to understand what he said—at least most of the time. But sometimes I get queasy when I hear people quote Jesus but do it out of context and with a meaning I am convinced the grammar could not allow. And I can't always tell if the distortion is inadvertent or deliberate. I ought not be too hard on them because I know I still might be twisting things. I don't intend to twist and distort his intent. However, I have learned enough about me to know it is difficult to eliminate my veneer of defensiveness with which I protect my faulty world view. Sometimes the truth hurts. My desire is to find the truth and follow it precisely. I am committed simply to allow Jesus to tune me up. I do want to be an accurate messenger and example who responds well to his teaching.

It is easy to skip by what he actually said and try to assign some adjusted meaning. It is important to settle the, "What did he say?" question first. Then logically we proceed to, "What does this mean?" Finally, "What difference does this make to me?"

It is easy to wander from his intentions and not see the difference his words demand. This is not a new problem. Once Jesus made a plain statement about responsibility to our neighbors. A religious leader got uncomfortable and asked a question. As Luke puts it, *"But he wanted to justify himself, so he asked Jesus, 'And who is my neighbor?'"* (Luke 10:29). Jesus responded with the story we call the Good Samaritan. But the religious leader was trying to get off the hook. Self-justification protects us from the truth. It is easier on our conscience if we simply avoid the issues and come up with what we think are tough questions. Then we can supply our own watered down version of an answer. In effect, we muzzle Jesus and jump in with our own inferior standards. We look for a diminished standard or loophole. We create our own little work arounds. We use the time honored tradition of asking the teacher questions to get the teacher off track so we won't get stuck with as much homework. We simply don't like the requirements Jesus sets so we attempt to develop a compromise.

Earlier I used the term "veneer of defensiveness." This is what I mean. There is an outer part of me that wants to ignore Jesus. I find that intuitively I want to change the instructions. I want to bring other points to bear. I want to pretend that my context is very different and therefore the teaching needs some serious adjustment. I want to believe that the expectations and clear demands were valid then because it was easier for them. A part of me wants to rationalize him out of my perceived world. I falsely think that it is more complicated now. Then things were pristine and simple. Now things are muddy and complex. Then the disciples didn't know as much. Now we know so much more. Then they didn't have the benefit of the rest of Scripture available on-line. Now we can cross reference things and have the benefit of 2000 years of theological studies.

As the slippery slope continues I am in danger of getting caught up in religious jargon, traditions and things that give momentary relief or exhilaration. I am also in danger falsely thinking the message needs to be upgraded. In this channel surfing world if I tell the whole truth people might reject it in a nano-second. People all around me think that Jesus is worn out. Others have got caught up in attempting to make Jesus cool. Some think we have to compete if we are going to get anyone to express loyalty to Jesus. Tools show up that the original disciples could not imagine.

Then they didn't have the benefit of several interpretations of the life of Jesus on the silver screen. Then they didn't have the surround-sound and the dynamic deep voice with various touches of digital audio enhancement. Then they didn't have the beautiful stunning architecture. Then they didn't have the stained glass. Then they didn't have the vestments and icons. Then they didn't have the impressive lighting and sound system. Then they didn't have the cameras and technology. Then they didn't have the soft rock band—errr, excuse me, Praise and Worship Team in the jargon of some. Then they didn't have 24 hour religious programming—and please keep the donations coming to keep this program on the air.

Then they didn't have a whole subculture built around the acceptable range of dress and defined meeting times to focus the religious obligations. Then they didn't have the weekly routine safely slotted into a particular start and finish time on one day of the week.

I understand why people throw the baby out with the bath water. So many want nothing to do with Christianity because of all the "noise." So many styles. So many approaches. So many interpretations. So many fakes. So many authoritarians who disagree with one another—even fight over it all.

In Jesus' day they had plenty of things to cloud their understanding. But they weren't distracted by a huge range of extraneous culture and information alleging to enhance the message of Jesus.

I am not advocating throwing away theological libraries or technologies. I am not saying that everything we do because it has become a routine has no value. I am not attacking any particular flavor of Christianity. I am not on the other hand advocating a, "We are all worshipping the same Guy" theology where we water down the message beyond its irreducible minimum.

In fact, if I am upset with any particular flavor it is the one I most identify with. I am most concerned about attacking the imperfections in my own world view. I want to make sure that I take the words of Jesus seriously. I want to come to the day when I can look him in the eye. I want to hear him say, "Pretty good, Gary. Pretty good."

As we begin together I am inviting you to join with me. Since we are going to spend some hours together can we agree on some simple ground rules?

Here is what I am asking you to say to yourself.

1. I am going to make sure Carter gives me the straight goods, even if it hurts. I want the actual concepts of Jesus not some cheap watered down or manipulated imitation.

2. I am going to give this book a fair hearing. Then I am going to consider adjusting my life if it makes sense to me, but only if it makes sense to me.

3. When I feel irritated, attacked or unjustly judged I am going to fight through it and listen carefully.

If you will agree to that as you listen, then I will agree to this as I speak.

1. I will not let myself say, "Yes but" and try to integrate what he said into my present world view and thus misrepresent what Jesus meant.

2. When Jesus says it, I'm going to believe it and adjust my life to live it out with abandonment.

3. I will let others question me and hold me accountable to behave according to what I write.

I don't want a fight. I especially don't want Jesus saying to me, "Wait a second Gar, that's not what I meant and you know it!"

I don't want you coming back at me and saying, "Wait a minute Gary, you didn't tell me the truth!"

Are you ready for the truth? Once we clear away some background issues in the next chapter we will be ready to take on specific statements from the mouth of Jesus. For many people, Simon and Garfunkel had it right in this couplet, "We're workin' our jobs, collect our pay / Believe we're gliding down the highway, when in fact we're slip sliding away." We need to take careful measure or the truth will simply slip on by.

"The time has come."

*Jesus
quoted in Mark 1:15*

3

It's Time!

It's time. The expectant mother wakes her mate up in the middle of the night. If it is her first, she's not exactly sure because her body has never done this before. She may have waited for an hour and let him sleep. But when she can't stand it any longer she taps him on the shoulder and says, "It's time."

From then on everything is a blur. The inevitable will occur. The mother's body must deliver this dearly loved foreign object. A child will be born. There is no turning back.

The text in the Bible that covers the life of Jesus is just under 10% of the total. In my favorite Bible that is 154 pages. Four different writers wrote this material. We call their four documents the four Gospels. In broad generalities, they all wrote their documents in the last half of the first century. Plenty of people were around to discredit their writing if it were not true. But that didn't happen. The first words out of Jesus' mouth as recorded by the four Gospel writers (Matthew, Mark, Luke and John) are different in every case. They actually start with four different events in Jesus' life. Probably Mark wrote his gospel first then Matthew and Luke and finally John. They all record precise events in Jesus' life. There are only 2 incidents recorded about Jesus' birth and one when he was about 12 years old. All the Gospels emphasize the final 3 years of his life and especially the events of the last week. Other than a few quotes from historians of the day this is all we know. But then again when for example, Josephus—a Jewish historian, gives us a few sentences on Jesus, we do affirm from non-biblical sources that Jesus is a historical character. Josephus was no fan—just a neutral historian. If you have a historical bent, Google "Josephus and Jesus" and "Tacitus and Jesus" and you will enter the zone of the historian. Not my zone. See ball. Hit ball. Remember?

For this book, all the material is based on a few quotes from the Gospel of Mark. You can find it by looking in the Table of Contents of any Bible you have. I would recommend you make sure it is a translation completed in the last 50 years or so and that you find a copy in large enough print so that it is pleasant to read. Failing that you can download Mark chapter by chapter and print it out for yourself from www.biblegateway.com. The accepted chapter and verse divisions in the Bible were not part of the original but have been in standard use for centuries. They make a handy way to find a particular sentence. Often the verses are little superscript numbers sprinkled throughout the middle of paragraphs. For that matter, the paragraphs and sentence divisions weren't part of the original text either. The document was written in common Greek which was pretty pervasive much like English is today. Mark told the whole story in about 14,000 words. This book will more than double that length. By all means, please take an hour and read Mark from top to bottom and get the whole story. In fact, I would encourage you to stop reading this and go do that first. Then you can come back here and see if I am picking out the material that captures the essence of what Jesus wanted those who were not yet his followers to know. That was the basis on which I selected the quotes we will examine.

"The time has come," he said. *"The kingdom of God is near. Repent and believe the good news!"* (Jesus quoted in Mark 1:15)

Wow! Do you see what a mouthful that is? Jesus certainly didn't sneak up on anybody. There is no, "Hi how are you? Are you having a nice day? Is this a good time to chat?" In fact, if you check out the other three Gospels you will see that even though they are starting at different points in his life, each of them starts with a strong and significant statement.

However, let us note from the beginning that it is clear we are getting the condensed version of what Jesus said whenever the Gospel writers record his statements. There are probably several reasons for this. One of the significant reasons is that in the first century everything that was recorded in writing had to be laboriously hand copied. That is a difference between then and now. I am writing this book in about one week using voice-recognition technology. It will be published within a few months with an unlimited number of copies available. Information dissemination was much different in Jesus' time. It was harder. And they needed to conserve words. But they did make every effort to be accurate. It is clear that Jesus wanted to get people's attention with significant content, not with any form of entertaining content. And by the way they did have lots of distractions to entertain in the New Testament era just like we do.

And while we are at it let's cover a commonly held error. It surprises me when people buy into this one. I think they learned it in the lunch room at high school or over a few beers in the pub at college. (Now that is a place to work out the meaning of the universe. Pool your ideas and see what consensus arises.) Here is the argument. "There are so many versions of the Bible and so many changes over the years we haven't any idea what Jesus actually said." They usually add something like this on the front end, "It is a proven scientific fact …" That ends all discussion. Ever heard that one? Sure you have. Did you ever ask for the source of that evidence? There is none. None. As a matter of record you can Google this one if you like; there are thousands of ancient hand written copies of Matthew, Mark, Luke and John that go way back hundreds of years before the printing press. These are used as the basis for every modern "version" of which I am aware. There is scarcely one word in 200 over which there is any textual variation at all. The word "version" doesn't mean different formations of the story. It simply means "translation." Take any translation you like as far as your pursuit is concerned. Or better get a bunch of them from the bookstore. You go ahead and figure out how much essential discrepancy there is for yourself. You will find the same message. You can't get off the hook with that ploy and be an intellectually honest person at the same time. Now let's get back to the facts here.

Let there be no doubt about it. Jesus had some things to say. When a house is on fire you don't knock on a door and say, "Excuse me, but if it is not too much trouble I think it may be useful for you to consider the possibility that there is an unusual occurrence of an incendiary nature happening with your domicile which you may wish to check out in due course." Urgency demands that you simply say, "Your house is on fire!" In fact, you had better put the appropriate urgency in your voice and on your face or your message may not be received.

It's time.

I'm going to use this next question a lot in this book so get used to it. What do you think Jesus meant when he said, *"The time has come?"* (Mark 1:15)

What time? Well, whatever time it is you can be sure that Jesus was pointing to a major shift. Whatever Jesus has to say to us, you can start with the assumption that he expects to frame things differently than you have ever known before. This is not a question of a midcourse correction. It is not a matter of learning a few optional principles that might, should you choose to employ them in your life, give you preferential treatment in time or eternity. Seems to be a, "Your house is on fire!" moment, doesn't it?

Further notice that he is not repeating something that has already been true in the universe. The grammar doesn't allow for that. You can't assume that Jesus is just stating the obvious. "Ho-hum. Yes, I knew that. The kingdom of God has always been near. I'm okay with that."

Bear in mind, Jesus is speaking largely to a Jewish audience. This Jewish audience in Palestine has an overlay of Roman political dominance and is heavily steeped in Greek culture. There are a whole bunch of world religions available to them in this cosmopolitan world. They are not naive. Jesus is not breaking on the scene as the first religious teacher. Jesus is not unaware of the world around him. And what he is saying is different. Very different. He is not saying here is a new option for you to consider. He uses the definite article *"the."* This is a unique and special time. That is what makes this information hot.

The key concepts in the full statement of Mark 1:15 are these. Now. Kingdom of God. Near. Repent. Believe. Good news. Agreed? Of course, he hasn't given us a whole lot of content for each of these concepts. But they are strong words. Therefore, they clearly stand in contradistinction to everything else that has gone on up until that point in history.

So you have the headlines. That ought to be enough to get you to read the story wouldn't you think? You can't accuse Jesus of wanting to blend in with the religious landscape.

So here we go. Right out of the box. Jesus is not a lobbyist. Jesus is not a negotiator attempting to bring all sides to an understanding of their common beliefs. He doesn't start with the premise that he will accept you no matter what. This is no image of a gentle-faced-arms-wide-open social worker who has come to provide comfort. This is a wake-up call. No, that's not strong enough. This is a house-on-fire call!

Jesus is on record and we are getting down to the hot brass tacks of it all. The concert has started. This is no gentle Brahms' lullaby. This is a bang bang, everybody on your feet, we are going to stir things up, rocking kind of event. If you take the challenge even to breeze through the events in the life of Jesus you are going to find bold statements, astounding events, radical demands, controversy and conflict. You are going to find an individual who was either an arrogant megalomaniac who should have been written off a long time ago or you are going to find something else. But one thing you are not going to find is some nice piece of religious art with everyone standing around with dreamy looks on their faces blindly admiring one individual in the center with a glowing aura and in stature a foot and a half above the quiet crowd.

It's time.

Procrastination is the thief of time. Sometimes delay is a good thing. It is important to make sure you don't simply act out of haste when you don't have to. If you are like me, and I suspect you are, you have made some really bad choices because you didn't think things through in advance. It might have been that you made some desperate life-altering choices that you deeply regret and you can now see that if you had only thought about it longer you would have taken a different course. At its extreme, we recognize that prisons are full of people who made a very bad snap decision. Thoughtful delay may be good. But just putting a decision off when we don't want to face the decision is not wise. If there is more information that needs to come to light then you have something to think about. But if there could not be any more important information no matter what. It's time.

I don't agree with this premise but you might think it is bad timing for you to alter your life course and follow Jesus. Even if I grant you plenty of delay time in coming to a final choice about Jesus, you would agree would you not, that doing your research now is a very good thing?

It's time to figure out what Jesus meant when he said, *"The time has come."* (Mark 1:15) Even if you reject it, it's worth a look, isn't it? It's time to figure out what Jesus meant by the *"kingdom of God."* Mark records the use of this term by Jesus 14 times. That has to be significant wouldn't you think? Why would you give a rip for what some guru says on a TV talk show until you get a handle on Jesus himself? It's time to figure out what Jesus meant when he said *"repent."* Why would you settle for the definition some stand-up comic provides? It's time to figure out what Jesus meant when he said *"believe."* Isn't it obvious that he wasn't simply talking about some general psychological mindset? It's time to figure out what Jesus meant when he said he had *"good news."*

If you grew up with any religion whatsoever, don't you think it is time to reach some adult decisions about what you were taught? And if you grew up without consideration of Jesus why would you accept that without personal evaluation? Are you one of those who is willing to accept without examination

It's Time!

the things you were taught about this? My experience shows that so many people have taken their definition of Jesus from some place other than the original documents. Many presume that it is too complicated to go back and figure this out on their own. How wrong that is. Some think the Bible is difficult to understand because they used a 400 year old translation as a child. Some think the Bible is difficult to understand because somebody said so. Others might tell you the story of the Bible is boring. How hard can it be to come to your own conclusion on that one? It will take you about an hour to read Mark from beginning to end. That is all I am asking you to do for now. You have probably spent more time watching reruns on television in the last week. Why not start from scratch? Why not find a quiet place and a Bible with decent sized print in a modern translation. I am using the New International Version but there are many others from which to choose. You don't have to get yourself an expensive leather bound version. Any inexpensive paper back will do. Virtually every bookstore has them. (If not, you might want to ask why not. The book is still the all time best seller, you know.) No excuses. It's time.

And, if you haven't taken a serious look at this message already, don't you think it's time to figure out when you are going to do that? Now is as good a time as any.

"The people were amazed at his teaching, because he taught them as one who had authority, not as the teachers of the law."

Mark 1:22

4

Moving Targets

Change keeps fiddling with my expectations. Technology is a fascinating arena in which change occurs at breakneck speed. One form of technology morphes into another faster than we ever dreamed earlier in our lives. Technologically speaking everything we purchase seems to become obsolete before we ever get to use up the warranty time on the previous technology.

It seems every time I visit the store I find a new invention I didn't know about before I entered the store. Then I leave the store thinking, "Me, I must get one of those for me ASAP!" Then by the time I get the car out of the parking lot, having resisted the urge to lay down the money, sanity kicks in and I ask myself, "If I didn't know about it before I entered the store, how can it be true that by the time I exited the store it got to my 'must have' list?" My list is a moving target. If I worked at it a little I think I could invest most of my time in revising my list.

When it comes to ultimate commitments in life I think we too easily develop a fear that something better might come along and we will be left with an old "tatoo" on our soul that is out of date and no longer meets our needs before we have completed the payment plan. Thus, the easy solution is to never make a commitment to anything because, like technology, it might wear out. While we know we can throw the technology away, we also know we would have a much harder time getting rid of the "soul tatoos." Even that "tatoo" illustration is wearing out fast because you actually can get a skin tatoo removed now—well, sort of. But that is not the point.

We all need some fixed points from which to calculate our life commitments. I recommend the words of Jesus as a wonderful place to start. Those words don't shift. They have formed the soul foundation for countless millions and they have formed my personal soul foundation. The last thing we need in life is a moving target for our starting point. A fixed starting point supplies comfort and clarity. But more importantly, if our fixed starting point is correct we are in much better shape than others without accurate information. Some new book or movie this year or next isn't going to deliver the answer as if it eluded us all until now. Yes, some new technology or advances will arrive this year or next; but holding out for a new solution to the problems of the universe is bound to meet with disappointment.

I firmly believe Jesus gave us the correct starting point, not just an alternative. Now I have to back that up and attempt to demonstrate it for you through the rest of this book. You may not agree; but at least you will know where I am starting from. I am asking you to seriously consider the message before you accept or reject it.

Before we go further into the precise statements of Jesus, let's take a step back and think about the documents I am recommending as the fixed starting point for unmasking life's meaning.

Jesus said it. He is on record. Matthew, Mark, Luke and John recorded it in the normal language of the day and location—Greek. Bible translators turned the Greek words into your language—presumably English since this is being written in English. There is a minimal amount of wiggle room between the original and the contemporary. There are literally thousands of handwritten copies of all or part of these documents still in known existence in libraries and museums around the world. These all predate the development of the printing press. There is a astounding degree of textual purity across the board. Most objective scientists in this area will attest to the fact that the textual variations with any significance at all make up about one half of one percent of the text. Imagine changing the message of a document by changing, at random, one word out of 200. Nobody could ever achieve that. There is little doubt about quality of the documentation. In contrast, a current author is attempting to discredit the message of the Bible based on 2—count them 2 (only)—alleged ancient documents. This author claims that the Vatican is keeping the lid on this. Need anyone take this attack seriously? Honest Bible translators don't get to do what speakers and writers sometimes do—put their own spin on things. Speakers interpret. Some writers speculate. Translators translate.

Translation is the science of meaning exchange from one set of words in one language to the same meaning in another language using an appropriate set of words. Honest translators make a sincere attempt to avoid distortion and adaptation as they translate. Thus translation, by its nature, is a science that resists adaptation. As the receptor language changes the translation changes of necessity to preserve the integrity of the words and concepts of the original language. A more modern translation is not more suspect because a translation doesn't by its nature change the original meaning; it attempts to get closer to the original meaning by using the best rendering of the most original text available and putting the meaning in the most current language available. You would be hard pressed to find any translation of the words of Jesus that has changed the essence of the meaning on a global basis. However, you might find some adaptation of the original meaning of a singular concept in a particular translation. So you are wise if you find a number of translations to compare and see if one of them wanders off from the group. It is rare. But in theory, it could happen.

Adaptation does get introduced into the mix when you get to the level of interpretation of the words. Any time someone undertakes to explain another person's words it is possible to move the meaning a teeny weeny bit. We all do it. I am really concerned that I don't do it as much as I hear some others doing it. I really want the original to speak. I want to get out of the way for you. Now, if I base my explanations on those I learned from others who in turn based their understanding on someone else's explanation I am in danger of making unwarranted adaptations. Theoretically, as one generation of thought builds on the previous this could get so far from the original that things get really out of hand. Thus, I encourage you to think hard and make sure I am not interjecting ideas that could create a tradition based on whims not facts.

Sometime you might hear someone using Jesus' precise words to back up their own ideas. For example, *"The truth will set you free."* (John 8:32) Whose truth is it anyway? Not the pot of watered down and sometimes poisoned soup being delivered but the truth as Jesus intended it. Give him a break. Don't just wheel out his words when you need an authority. And don't you let me misrepresent him either. See ball. Hit ball. Pitchers spin the ball. Jesus wasn't into spin. He gave it to us direct enough so we could handle it, if and only if we have our ears tuned in his direction.

While there might be some range for interpretation in some cases, my intention is to avoid fiddling with the middle ground. I want to explore the meaning of plain statements made by Jesus. He alleged that the things he said are true.

To suggest that what he says is really only true if you believe it so is a handy way to avoid dealing with what he said. I want to expose your individual life to these personal statements of Jesus without any formalized expression of religion in the room. I will avoid the middle ground created by my personal background, traditions and circle of human relationships. I cannot eliminate it completely because I am imperfect in my understanding. But I think we can do better together on this if we try to stick to basics.

These words are going to challenge some of your deeply held beliefs. You can believe whatever you choose. But you don't get to define truth. If Jesus was telling the truth, it is the truth regardless of what you have been led to believe. Jesus speaks in absolutes. If you believe truth is relative you may find Jesus' words irritating. Can you handle that?

There are some things that are relative truth. That is, what is true for you might be different for me. There are also some things that are true whether or not either you or I believe them. Just because some have taken their relative ideas and foisted them off on us as absolutely true when they were not gives us no license to say that everything must be relative. Frankly, there have been so many add-ons to Christianity that some find it difficult to sort it out. For example, Christmas is deemed to be a Christian holiday. Did you know that Christmas is almost a complete fabrication by people over time? Jesus had nothing to do with that. It is quite certain that his birth stories were not celebrated at all among early followers. I don't care to trash all Christmas traditions but I do intend to blow on by incidentals like that and get to the essentials. How one celebrates Christmas is relative. What Jesus said is foundational. The absolute truth is all that really counts here.

In every generation young people start off with a "who says?" attitude. I happen to think that is a very good thing if managed properly. But when it degenerates to a "nobody tells me what to believe or do because I get to decide what is true for me" attitude it gets dicey. I find some who sincerely hold this view get a rude awakening when a baby comes along. The baby believes in absolute truth. When Baby gets hungry it isn't relative. You can say, "Baby, wait until I feel hungry" if you like. But it won't last long. Baby wins. Young adult begins to adjust philosophy of life. Relativism starts to melt into a world of absolute realities.

When you were young you lived with imposed standards in many areas and probably had little trouble with most of them. "Say, 'Please.'" "Say, 'Thank you.'" "Tell your sister, 'I'm sorry.'" That got harder but you said it anyway. As you grew, in moral areas you might have found the world getting complicated. Perhaps you grew up in a world where you were trained not to tell lies except when it was convenient. In response to a telephone ring, "Tell them I'm not home." In response to a habit, "Don't do as I do; do as I say." Those in authority upset your moral compass with multiple standards. That made it hard for you to figure things out. There is room for disagreement with many things in life. But there is a big difference between the choice of the color of the clothes you wear and the things that deeply affect your personhood. How those who parented you lived shouted much louder than their voice. Who you become is much more caught than taught.

It is really damaging when the authority figure hides behind a cloak of moral authority and brings religion to their aid to support standards to restrict you when in fact those standards have been arbitrarily set based on their own convenience or tradition. Things that should have been relative might have been portrayed as absolute. Things you should have been allowed to figure out on your own, albeit with some guidance, might have been imposed. That might have been convenient for the authority. It might have been intended to save you some trouble but it messed with your autonomy and the development of your own moral compass. You may have made the mistake of trying some things you should have left alone just because you wanted to figure it out on your own. There is after all a delicate and individual balance few of us find in helping another human develop. That delicate balance requires affirming the person's desire to choose freely and accepting our responsibility to protect those in our care. If the previous generation got it wrong we are prone to over react to another extreme.

Sometimes the standards set for us were ridiculous without solid foundations. Someone imposed their standards on us as absolutely true when they were not. However, that gives us no license to say that therefore everything must be relative. We may need to redraw the line between absolute and relative. We may need to leave a larger zone of uncertainty between the things that are non-negotiably true and the things where some might approach things differently. Frankly, in the pursuit of God there are different opinions. What various systems put in the absolute category is variable. It is obvious that different religious approaches see things differently.

I deeply desire to transcend any and every set of religious roots and just get back to the basics. I want you to join me in that pursuit. That means that if you have a nonreligious viewpoint, you and I should get along just fine here. Frankly, I want to convert you to Jesus' explanation of the things we will look at. He was not a relativist as you will soon discover. He made definite statements without ever saying the equivalent of, "I could well be wrong, but from my perspective ..." He never came even close to suggesting, "This might change as the generations pass but for now ..." When you read it over you won't find him leaning on his human heritage for his content. And you certainly won't find him relying on the people around him to shape his viewpoint. I want you to watch to see if these premises are true in the statements of Jesus we study. But please go ahead and read everything he said. Other than one short concept from the book of Acts, everything we have that was recorded about what he did say is recorded in Matthew, Mark, Luke or John. For our purposes, we are going to stick to Mark. This is one way in which we will take a "See Ball; Hit Ball" attitude.

Specifically, we are going to park on one huge mouthful for a few chapters here. And this is no moving target. We already started with the first four words, *"The time has come"*. (Mark 1:15) Jesus was not suggesting it might be time; he was definite. There is no wiggle room there as far as he is concerned. What if he is telling the truth?

The whole statement including those four words is a mere sixteen words in the English translation I am using. *"The time has come, the kingdom of God is near. Repent and believe the good news!"* (Mark 1:15) But these sixteen words might just be all you need to yank your chain and turn you in a whole new direction. And the promise is a wonderful direction indeed. Curious? I certainly hope so! Let's get to it.

*"The kingdom of God
is near."*

*Jesus
quoted in Mark 1:15*

5

Good Government

History shows us that nations come and go. That is difficult for us to grasp because we live in the moments of our own generation and easily forget the past. We do not like the instability created when political regimes change. In the past generation we have witnessed many domineering political systems come crumbling down. Even within a stable Western democracy nervousness is aroused when a different political party wins an election.

In the current global political landscape we are not really fond of kings—particularly autocratic ones. However, we may create some political space for them as figureheads. It gives some countries someone permanent to point to as the theoretical leader. And at least the royal family doesn't change every few years like elected governments do.

In a few minutes we are going to change the paradigm radically as we consider a whole different kind of kingship and control. But first I would like to say a bit about my situation.

I am a Canadian. Many are not aware that technically speaking our country is a constitutional monarchy. Our head of state is also the monarch of Great Britain. We actually have a representative of the monarch who moves around our country making speeches and cutting ribbons for state occasions. But—shhhh there may be some committed monarchists listening—that one we call the Governor General is deemed to be mostly irrelevant by many, if not most, of the citizens. And we have Lieutenant Governors in all our provinces. By the way, that is pronounced "LEF tenant."

Yes, there are some kings and queens in this world who actually run their countries but that is not a common affair anymore. The lofty ideal of a king of regal bearing, fine moral character and fair judicial mind as protector and manager of a country with loyal subjects might show up in some medieval movie but not much in real life.

So when Jesus uses the term, *"kingdom of God"* (Mark 1:15) it doesn't exactly send chills down anyone's spine—at least not in the West in this generation. However, there is enough residual awareness of kingship for the average person to warm up to the term a little bit. It's not hard. A king is a king of a realm. So this has something to do with God being in charge of something.

God is in charge. Of something. It is common to admit God is in charge of all the things that don't go well. So when disappointment strikes somebody mumbles something about, "God's will." Natural disaster strikes. Oops—God must have been in charge since clearly it is beyond the ability of humankind to control it. Sometimes we mask this fatalism a little bit with a statement like, "It was not meant to be." We may not put God in the sentence but if you were going to supply a subject for that sentence who else could you pick? Your other option might be some undefined deterministic force that is in charge of the cosmos. It might be sort of like gravity with a bit of a mind and a plan. You might even come up with a series of deterministic forces or wills which remain unseen and perhaps even nameless. But the reality is you don't get to determine who is in charge of what. This isn't a game played in a doll house where one kid gets to decide who the Daddy is. You can play whatever comforting games you please and pretend you can define the roles in the universe. That might give you the illusion of control. But it won't give you real control.

I think it is really interesting that people are very happy to point a finger in God's direction for all the bad stuff and perhaps even some of the good stuff. But other than the big events he gets left out of life's equations. They may give some form of lip service to a belief in God but don't even give him reference in day-to-day life. Isn't that like someone who says they are deeply devoted to art but don't have any pieces hanging on their walls nor visit any art galleries?

If there is any content in Jesus' words, you have got to get the picture that this kingdom of God which is near is not some passive general acknowledgment of God's place in the world. Jesus breaks on the scene with his bold statement. Obviously, he didn't think he was breaking into the party to announce the score to the game of life when everybody already knew the outcome. It is pretty clear that this proclamation was in fact something of significance that up until now was unannounced. It was not a generally accepted concept. Clearly nobody knew the score.

So if this is a big announcement what could be involved? Let's consider the text. We already know that, *"The time has come."* (Mark 1:15) This isn't necessarily time in the sense of clock time. It could be time in the sense of the opportune moment. Either way, it is the right time for something new. *"The kingdom of God is near."* (Mark 1:15) This realm where God is in charge is near. It is just around the corner. It is coming down the street. If there is even the remotest chance that Jesus is telling the truth, anyone with normal human faculties ought to be excited about that parade!

Think for a moment. What if this proclamation of *"the good news of God"* (Mark 1:14) by Jesus is in fact a life-changing, society-building, family-nurturing and universe-fulfilling concept? What if this wasn't like another overblown commercial on a new product that couldn't deliver as promised? What if at that precise moment this singular good news item coming from a unified singular source is now available for free to anyone who listens? What if this is a message coming from beyond the earth to the ears of the world of people? What if what the Gospel writer John said is true? *"The Word became flesh and made his dwelling among us. We have seen his glory, the glory of the One and Only, who came from the Father, full of grace and truth."* (John 1:14) And what if the kingship of this Word was absolutely perfect—giving people everything they were truly looking for? What if, as abused humans, this take-matters-into-my-own-hands-because-I-can't-trust-anyone attitude we all develop could be suspended in favor of a system where we are protected, nurtured, developed and cared for by the perfect king?

A key point of resistance for some is the very notion that they should have to submit to anyone or thing. They work around the government. Vote. Complain. Vote again. Complain bitterly whenever taxes go up. Disbelieve all election promises and then vote for the party with the best promises only to have hopes dashed once more. They work around the company. They show up on time because they have to. They do as little work as possible to still come away with a pay check. Or they work like crazy to get promoted. Eventually submitting to the company wears so many out. They discover the company doesn't really care. They work around family demands. Their spouse is not the person they married. It escapes them that that cuts both ways. Their children are ungrateful. Some have a discouraging road. If, on that road, one sees paying attention to Jesus as just another set of imposed obligations or a place to experience dashed hopes, it would be a normal response to say, "Who needs it?"

The best approach seems to be avoidance until the next explosion. The problem is that life is so daily. The demands keep flowing. Oh, I know it isn't that bad for everyone nor all the time. But when you think about it you realize that people aren't looking for a new king. They have enough kings in their life as it is. Managing life under their existing kings is quite a job.

This good news changes everything. It offers the kingdom of God to straighten all things out for time and eternity! This is really, really good news. Doesn't it boggle your mind that people will claim to be followers of Christ and never get excited about anything to do with him? Doesn't it raise a credibility problem when someone says in effect, "Yep I have my membership card in my hip pocket. My parents bought it for me. Now leave me alone."

About 2000 years after this inaugural declaration many more people than not think the concept is faulty or suspect because we don't see God and ideals we associate with him operating around us. I get that. It eats me up most days of my life. The issue here isn't impotence in the message. The problem is that more people who say they believe the message don't actually restructure their lives to live it and spread it.

When we get this right, it is not like showing up to some state occasion where there is the glitter, pomp and circumstance of a state occasion because the Lieutenant Governor or monarch is in town. The event comes. The event goes. It creates a slice of life and some interesting memories. But it doesn't change anything. No. No! This idea of God taking over for our good is full of lasting energy and hope.

What do you think Jesus meant when he said, *"The time has come. The kingdom of God is near."*? (Mark 1:15) Wouldn't the next sentence about how to get in on it be important? Wouldn't you turn up the volume and tell everyone to be quiet because these are the moments you have been waiting for?

> *"Repent and believe the good news!"*
>
> *Jesus*
> *quoted in Mark 1:15*

6

Twin Essentials

When somebody tells me there are only two rules to learn I respond with two thoughts. The first thought is, "Great this should be easy." The second is, "It can't be that simple; you are trying to trick me."

But sometimes I admit things can be summed up in two rules. Have you heard of these two rules for life? Rule #1: Don't sweat the small stuff. Rule #2: Everything is small stuff. I am not sure that applies everywhere but I have found it useful to keep my focus at times.

I love infomercials. Once in a while they hook me and I buy. But not usually. I just like watching how they try to reel me into their boat. It goes like this. They tell you what a great product they have and how it solves some big problem. Usually it makes your life simple, fast and efficient. It's all you really need. They convince you of the value. You could pay hundreds of dollars for a variety of equipment to do the tasks this one amazing tool will do for you. But they don't tell you the price yet. They go back to reinforcing how good this gizmo is. Oh yes, they sprinkle in lots of testimonies from satisfied users. The host is way too enthusiastic. The studio audience—only a fool would believe they are just a random bunch of participants—is made up of all the kinds of people that can benefit from this great product. Also, they are way too pumped. But they look just like you—only prettier. Eventually they tell you the price. It seems reasonable. Only four easy payments. Then we get to the bonuses. And then the "But wait, if you call in the next 18 minutes we will make one payment for you. And we will double your order!"

Whatever.

By the end of the half hour they have me laughing at myself. I find myself believing that I actually want and even need this product.

In the end I believe this might just be a great product and it represents exceptional value. Sort of like the two rules thing. Great product. Great price. What more could I ask? I didn't know I needed it until a half hour ago. Now I can't live without it.

But usually that little red skeptic light in the back of my brain starts flashing before they get my credit card number. Will I really use it? Does it actually work as advertised? Will they actually be there to make good on that lifetime guarantee? Is it more important that I spend money on this or something else instead? That red light has been well polished. Normally, I pay attention to it.

You have one of those don't you? One of those little red skeptic lights? Very useful device. It can save you a lot of money and embarrassment. When you are young it doesn't work as well but it gets better over time for most of us. The problem is as I see it, as the struggles of life pile up many up the wattage too far. They become too skeptical in general and don't apply discernment appropriately.

Many seem to think there is a quota for struggles that one has to pay and then the good times roll. It is something like initiation rites to get into a campus fraternity. It is gruesome to get through it but you hear that the parties on the inside are well worth it. I hope you have it figured out by now that is not the way it works. You are bound to have what you think is more than a fair share of trouble in life. It will comfort you a little to think of all the people who are worse off. But that won't take your trouble away. It will comfort you little to tell yourself that things will work out if you keep a positive approach. There is no doubt a positive approach has some value. But a positive approach won't delay or diminish much of your trouble. And a brighter red skeptic light is no solution. In fact, it will lose you friends. Nobody likes to be around a person who reminds them of all negative possibilities and has nothing positive to recommend.

You need solutions. Of course, if you have lowered your standards to the place where you aren't looking for any more solutions, you can develop a measure of tranquility. But you will be boring and unattractive if you do. And besides—and this is the big issue—maybe that approach can get you from here to the grave, but it won't solve your problem with eternity. Why would you take a chance that the grave ends it all if there is even the remotest possibility there is a Maker to face? You don't like that level of risk do you? For goodness sake, you probably change your batteries in your smoke alarms twice a year just in case. And it is likely that the worst fire you will ever face in your house is burnt toast. When it comes to eternity everyone needs a solution.

The common viewpoint suggests that if there is a life after death with an upside usually called heaven, you get there by being good. Most people figure they are good enough. When we stand back we can find the good in almost anybody. We seem compelled to lower our version of the entrance requirements to heaven until their is room for all. We hate to contemplate the hard cold truth in the face of grief. Now it may not be the best time to point the truth out at the funeral and it is too late anyway. But pretending to lower the entrance requirements for someone else doesn't change reality. If the entrance requirement were how good we live on earth, our ability to objectively measure would be suspect indeed. The be-good-enough-and-you-will-make-it premise is totally flawed for a number of reasons. But at least, we can all agree on this, there could never be a fairly applied standard across the globe if it were left to the vote of any bunch of people. Further, we can all agree that if we are left to set the bar for ourselves we all make it to heaven. Even disgusting criminals will make it because they say they are good enough. But that whole discussion about good lives and bad has nothing to do with Jesus' statements about how to get to the kingdom of God. According to Jesus, the common viewpoint is just plain wrong. If you are struggling with that, put a mental bookmark on the concept and listen to what Jesus has to say as we uncover it—at least some of it—through the rest of this book.

Jesus teaches us about reality. In a few pages we are going to hear what Jesus has to say about the live-a-good-life-and-get-to-heaven theory. But first, we need to look at the real entrance requirements.

What if there are only two things you need to do to get positively plugged into the kingdom of God? If someone were to come along and tell you about only two things you needed to do would you believe it? Or would the glare from that little red skeptic light keep you from even considering the possibility? Would you just retreat into the answers your heritage supplied—whatever they might be—or would you take a look? It is easy to fall back on, "Mamma always told me ..." And much of what Mamma said was good. But not perfect. What if on the really big issues Mamma was wrong? You would take a look just in case, wouldn't you?

There is a solution. That is exactly what Jesus proposed. *"Repent and believe the good news."* (Mark 1:15) Done. Could it really be that simple? See ball. Hit ball.

Two words that twin themselves together; you can't have one without the other and you have to apply them in the correct direction. But yes, that simple. At least, that is what Jesus appears to be alleging. Listen carefully once again. *"The time has come. The kingdom of God is near. Repent and believe the Good News!"* (Mark 1:15) Okay so that is just an outline; but what an outline!

Notice the range of information words there. *"The time has come."* (Mark 1:15) The audience had a special appreciation for that. They were looking for the right moment when God would jump in and get some saving done. *"The kingdom of God."* (Mark 1:15) That is a biggee. But there is no mistaking that Jesus is tying himself into the concept. There is also no disclaimer like "perhaps" or "it seems to me...." He is very definite. *"Is near."* (Mark 1:15) That could be near in time or space or both, but for sure it is not far away. That is all foundational information. But we must get beyond information and ask, "So what?" There are only two words in there that create application and supply the answer. And clearly, without those two words there is no deal. Those two words destroy the be-good-and-you-will-make-it-to-heaven theory. The two words are *"repent"* and *"believe."* (Mark 1:15)

You have heard the word "believe" often enough. People can do amazing feats when they psych themselves up for it. Chemistry can do wonders in the body. I am not a scientist or endocrinologist but I do know that adrenaline junkies love the rush they get from whatever turns them on. And I know that when happy little endorphins get running around in one's brain it is easy to feel no pain. Any stage hypnotist knows how to make this work. Many people attribute such natural hormonal responses to the special intervention of God. In my view, that approach, as sincere as it might be really cheapens the message—but that is for another day. This is not about getting a rush of hormones or setting aside all other options in favor of a single-minded focus that gets something done. You know what? You can walk over hot coals and not get burned. And if you take the right course it will give you the courage to focus enough to do it. But why would you need that? You could come to the place where you believe that fire walking is a metaphor for life. You could get yourself so pumped that you believe you could do anything you decided to do. But you would be wrong. You have your limits. Probably you can get a whole lot more out of life by breaking down false walls in your belief system but you can't do anything. Sorry. That is just silly.

Think about the word *"believe"* (Mark 1:15) as Jesus is using it—not the way it is used in common culture. Jesus always points the word *"believe"* in a direction. The direction is always to himself and the *"good news"* (Mark 1:15) message he is sharing. The belief is never pointed towards the inner self. There is so much on the bookstore shelves and the talk show circuit that invites you to look to your deeper self. In fact, much of it says if you will look deep enough into your soul you will find God there. Would you care for a second opinion? Let's see if this is what Jesus said. *"The time has come. The kingdom of God is near."*

(Mark 1:15) (So far so good …) "Look inside and find the good news!" NOT! Folks, if you look inside honestly you won't find good news. You will find worth. You might find comfort in a system that seem to be good news. But there is a repurposing and refining of your person and direction before anything meets the standard of *"good news"* (Mark 1:15) as defined by Jesus. His *"good news"* (Mark 1:15) is very attainable and not hard to find!

This is the fabulous message. You don't have to play a game. No amount of extreme makeover is going to get it done. You don't have to pretend anymore! Jesus invited people to *"believe the good news!"* (Mark 1:15) We don't have much content for that yet. We will get to that. But for now let the record show that Jesus' message was that people have to get their belief pointer headed straight before they get the whole package they are longing for.

The other word is the "R" word. This is the one people don't like. They have a hard time fitting this into the "god inside me" notion. *"Repent and believe."* (Mark 1:15) One out of two won't cut it. If you don't like that concept, you will have to take it up with Jesus; I am just the messenger.

So, other than some cartoon with a long-bearded old nut case walking down Main Street with a sandwich board sign and the word "Repent!" emblazoned on it, what does that word bring to mind? Do you conjure up a picture of someone having an emotional breakdown crying in despair?

It might surprise some to learn that is not it. Actually, the word repent is not an emotional one at all. Its basic meaning is "change of mind." The concept here is simply a deliberate choice to change your internal compass from the self-directed base you started with and turning your thoughts, intentions, behaviors and personhood towards something else. In this case, that turning is towards believing the *"good news."* This isn't about joining some religion. This is about starting a new relationship with following Jesus. We will get to that later. But for now let's leave it with this. Jesus clearly expected that those who were interested in the kingdom of God and its acquisition would in fact need to do two things, *"Repent and believe the good news."* (Mark 1:15)

Of course, Jesus was originally saying these words in earshot of a small crowd. But at the end of the book Mark has him telling his very few committed followers to get this good news message out to all creation. We are still working on that. And so the message is coming down through the centuries with exactly the same words and impact as it did nearly 2000 years ago. This is no cheap, fly by night operation here. I will grant you that there is a lot of garbled misdirection of this message. For example, perhaps you heard some preacher say, "Just believe in Jesus." Sorry. That is all good if you really understand that believing and repenting are two sides of one coin. But if you leave the repenting out you drop the level of meaning in the word "believing" below the threshold Jesus set.

Don't get hung up thinking this repenting and believing is a distasteful affair. Remember, from Jesus' perspective this is really good news for you! The good news is that you can *"repent and believe"* and thus get in on *"the kingdom of God."* While the message was delivered near a lake in what some call the Holy Land nearly 2000 years ago, it is clear by what Jesus says elsewhere that the message will not be rescinded and will reach its culmination when he comes a second time. We aren't going to deal with that promise in depth in this book. But his promise to return does set the backdrop to affirm that the message is still hot today. He is not diminished if you don't get it. But you sure are! So take a deep breath. Turn. Turn from whatever holds your allegiance and turn to the good news! You will wonder how you ever got along without it after you get it. You will never even imagine asking for your money back!

*"Come, follow me
and I will make you fishers
of men."*

*Jesus
quoted in Mark 1:17*

7

Go Fishing

Do you remember your first job? I certainly do.

It was in the advertising field. Well okay, it was a day worker job with a flyer distribution company called "Accurate Distribution." That sounded very official to me. My mother got me the job. I was very grateful—that is before I actually did the job. I thought she had to pull some strings to get me in.

Before sunrise on the first day I realized I wasn't going to start in a glass office tower with a corner unit and potted plant in the corner by the floor to ceiling window. I nervously walked into the garage-like space. I felt like there were a thousand seedy eyes on me as I walked up to the window and gave my name.

They herded about a dozen of us into the back of a windowless panel truck and off we went. I worked hard all day going door-to-door diligently placing a flyer at every door as I had been instructed to do. As the day wound down I realized getting rich doing this was going to be a challenge. Others however, had found some ways to improve their chances. As the tough supervisor drove around he knew to check the culverts and garbage bins. To my astonishment he found hundreds of undistributed flyers. It shocked me. I didn't know that people would cheat like that.

I had put in an honest day's work for about a half day's pay. I didn't last a week. I didn't get paid very much but then I didn't have to pay them for the education either.

Work shapes us. Men in particular tend to describe themselves by their occupations. Every job I've ever had has taught me something. As I think about it, I do count those first few days at the misnamed Accurate Distribution Company as a valuable start in a life which has been invested in information distribution. After all these years nothing has changed one of the lessons learned on my first day of work. It ain't easy to get the information out there.

When Jesus began recruiting his information dissemination group he used their vocational background as well.

Jesus didn't start with what we now call the white-collar crowd. He recruited men who knew what it was to put in a day working with their hands and sometimes coming home wondering what they had accomplished. He began with fishermen. Just like it ain't easy to get the information out there, it ain't easy to get the fish in the boat every day.

So the message for them was full of meaning, *"Come. Follow me. I will make you fishers of men."* (Mark 1:17)

That seems pretty straightforward. But let's unpack it carefully. The first thing I want you to notice is that Jesus is making an alternative vocational offer to them which uses their résumés. The lesson here seems to be that Jesus was interested in taking what they were and repurposing it at a higher level. This is no longer about smelly fish.

We can learn a lot about Jesus and his intentions for people by thinking about what he didn't say. He didn't start by offering a happier life. He didn't begin by offering them a home in heaven. He didn't offer them a religious alternative. He started by offering them a job. He didn't even use the forgiveness of sins as an opener. He started by recruiting them to invest their time with him, and with him in charge. He implied he would become their mentor. It is interesting that some think this offer is for a special group of people who were to become the equivalent of modern day paid clergy. No. It was an offer directly to a few to set the standard of Jesus' offer to all.

First and foremost in the offer of Jesus to people is his offer of a relationship. Now that's a little easier to understand when you have a flesh and blood Jesus and some sweaty fishermen beside a lake. The picture is tangible. But if we attempt to translate those first century initial events into today's terms where we cannot see Jesus, it gets a little more metaphysical. Today, when I say I have a relationship with Christ the imagery shifts but the essence is the same. I follow him. That is to say, I pay very close attention to what Jesus asked of his followers. I accept those requirements for my own life and I commit myself to live by his standards. I wish I was better at it. I mess up frequently. But there is never a day that goes by when I don't remember something he expects of me and deliberately attempt to behave in such a way that he will be proud of me.

I suppose some of those behaviors have become ingrained and more or less automatic. I'm not aware of that if it is true. But then, have you ever noticed how people who have been married to each other for quite some time get to look like each other? Try it sometime. Go into a public place and play a matching game. Even when couples are at opposite ends of the store you can make an educated guess as to who belongs to whom. I don't think they are aware of how much they look the same. But you are aware. In the same way, those who seriously walk with Jesus don't carry themselves as if they had been walking with the aloof upper crust. They look like people without ulterior motives but with a purposeful positive agenda.

What do you think Jesus meant? He said, *"Come. Follow me."* (Mark 1:17) It is pretty easy to figure out that he didn't mean that he was going to start a relationship where he would follow you around like a butler ready to meet your every need. I get nervous when I hear people talk about life with Christ and it all seems to be as if he is there for them. The first order of business when you follow is to get your boots on and move. The path is defined by the leader not the follower. It is the follower's job to get in step with the leader. His direction. His pace. His agenda. His road map.

When church people are surveyed and asked about their activities on a day-to-day basis which fulfill their followership requirements, some interesting facts emerge. Most everyone says they pray every day. Very few people say they consult the road map every day. Isn't that interesting? All we have left to give us direct instruction about how to live, where to go, who to relate to and how to relate to them is clearly defined for us in the total message of the Bible as endorsed by Jesus who said *"the scripture cannot be broken."* (John 10:35) In particular, since we are focusing on the life of Jesus in this book, we learn about him, his intentions and concerns in Matthew, Mark, Luke and John. Read the instructions. Don't go asking him to give you new instructions. Read them. Follow them. Don't debate them. See ball. Hit ball. Don't make this complicated. Those who want to follow Jesus take what he said and do it. No questions asked.

The nature of following Jesus is clearly framed for us. Everything we do when we are following him closely takes as its primary reference point from fishing for people. Now perhaps that imagery seems a little dehumanizing for some. But come on; give Jesus a break. Even today we talk about vocational recruiters as "headhunters." And if the job is right, today people brag when a "headhunter" calls. The idea here is not about turning people into fish; it is about applying the same sort of study, skill, effort and experience to finding new followers for Jesus as the fisherman has to apply to get fish into his boat. The fish are out there. The people are out there. The fish don't bite every day. The people don't respond every day. The fish don't jump into the boat. The people don't find Jesus on their own. The parallels go on and on. The grammar clearly requires a connection between two activities. Follow and fish. Don't follow and fishing is irrelevant. Don't fish and you are not following. Making a decision to follow Jesus is not simply a decision to get a valid passport to the next life. This is not about an exit strategy for life after death. It is a to do list for life before death.

It is quite clear that when Jesus recruited people he met their needs by teaching them how to recruit other people. The primary activity required of disciples in every generation is fishing. The technical term from a theological perspective is evangelism. That might be a scary word but literally it is a word that was invented in English to cover the precise concept in the original Greek of "spreading the good news." But "goodnewsing" just didn't cut it for a translation. The first order of business as far as Jesus was concerned was to get the Good News out there. He demonstrates throughout the rest of the Gospel of Mark and the other Gospels how much reaching new people mattered to him. He was driven to find new people. It is impossible to follow him closely and not have the same burning desire to reach and win new people. Now definitely, God created people to relate to him and others who love him. We simply don't do well on our own. We need to respond with our inner and outer beings in devotion to God. We have the privilege of ingesting accurate information to reshape our thinking and behavior. We get to enjoy comforting and energizing relationships with the extended family of God. We are provided the fulfilling opportunity to serve others. All of these things count. Simply put, you cannot have a complete life without each of these elements. But the first item on his agenda is "goodnewsing."

Perhaps you have purchased this book or received it is a gift with the understanding that you are considering what it means to become a follower of Jesus Christ. I want to give you a word of advice about all of this. Should you decide that Jesus is your new mentor there will be some radical changes start to emerge in your life from the inside out. You will do best at those changes if you unite with a group of people who are also on a journey making the same set of changes. For example, you can fish alone but it is better if you do it with others. It is hard to have a meaningful discussion in your own head. You tend to just rearrange your prejudices instead of actually improving your ideas. And besides, it is just more fun to have someone to talk to about a subject in which you are interested.

Pick your group carefully. Make sure they are following Jesus. But if you just ask, "Are you following Jesus?" you will likely get a hurt look along with a vociferous affirmative answer. How could you ever doubt us? Ahh, but look harder than that. Is their behavior consistent with the mind of Jesus? For example, do they care about fishing? Do they fish? Do they invest money in fishing gear? If they didn't do that last year it is not likely they will do it this year. If they haven't caught many fish in the last two years how hard are they trying? Are they actually putting a net in the lake? Or do they just like to take classes on how to put a net in the lake? If there are no nets in the lake, no fishing is going on. Why would you want to try to learn how to fish from people who don't fish?

Here are some points to bear in mind while you are thinking about these fishing groups. These people cluster together in more or less strongly knit groups. People come and go in these groups which are built on the premise of voluntary association. However, these groups of people properly formed have an enduring quality to them even though people move in and join while others move away.

These groups of people exist in virtually every place on the globe. There is no sociological structure anywhere that is as pervasive and universal as these groups of people. In many cases, because of their circumstances, they meet in meager surroundings. Sometimes they meet out of doors in designated locations in the woods. Other groups meet in homes. Still others rent facilities such as public libraries and schools. Yet again other groups construct buildings in which to meet. In many places around the world those buildings are very basic since they are constructed with semiskilled volunteer labor. The materials normally are purchased locally with locally donated dollars. Sometimes on the other end of the scale, these buildings are quite spectacular. But they are still constructed entirely by donations and in some cases the return on investment of saved donations. On rare occasions there is a level of coercion applied to generate these donations. Those circumstances are exceptional. In the vast majority of cases the money comes from people who voluntarily donate without any agency forcing them to do so.

Isn't that something? Millions and millions of places around the world built entirely on a volunteer basis with no national media campaign to raise the money. Often the word "church" is applied to these buildings. Technically, that is a total misuse of the word "church." That is a word that belongs to the group of people not the building. It is just like other groupings of people. A particular club might own its own building but the building is not the club; it is the club house. The original Greek word for "church" was borrowed from normal language. It was an assembly of people who met regularly for a particular purpose such as the meetings of a political party. The word was adopted to refer to the people who gathered together for the purpose of motivating each other to follow Jesus and fish.

These groupings of people that we call churches sometimes organize themselves into clusters known as denominations or fellowships. Each of these is structured differently with their own names. Even the familiar denominational names are used by many different unrelated groups. They all have their own flavor and style. Seldom is there any interest in competing with one another and certainly not in destroying each other. It is by and large a friendly and cooperative system. These groups are not like rival gangs trying to usurp each other's territory. There is plenty of room for all of them. Now as you consider your own relationship to this incredible array of possible places to plug into you might have some homework to do.

Here are some tips. Just because the group seems like they are nice people doesn't necessarily mean they are nice people who are passionate about following Jesus.

There is a wide range of styles available. Don't get hung up on style without being sure of the substance.

You may have heard or even experienced a horror story with one group or individual who identified with a particular denominational flag. That doesn't mean everyone using the same flag is that way.

Just because somebody says they follow Jesus in their group doesn't mean that they actually take the words of Jesus seriously. I would think that you would desire to join a group where the trappings are minimized, thus reducing the risk of getting hung up on the trappings and missing the essence of following Jesus.

The group of people you identify with as followers of Jesus may or may not be the same group of your heritage. For example, if you have sincere parents who saw it one way and you now see it a different way that you are convinced will give you more traction in following Jesus, you show your parents no disrespect by moving to a different group. They wanted the best for you. Find the best. Changing denominations to align more closely with Jesus and the Bible is an honorable pursuit. This is not like turning your back on your ethnicity or even citizenship. You couldn't change your ethnic roots if you wanted to. You probably have no interest in changing your citizenship and you can't change your country of origin. But you can choose the people with whom you will build relationships. And thus, you can choose your church.

Don't let your decision become clouded with a bunch of emotional baggage. Look for the facts. Look for a group that can help you follow Jesus wholeheartedly should you ultimately make the decision to accept the good news.

We are a long way into the book and really only a few words into the words of Jesus. That is because Jesus' words are full of significance and meaning. Keep a precise focus on what he meant. Don't let your understanding go mushy because of all the distractions. Why not make a decision right now to find a group of people and start fishing?

"It is not the healthy who need a doctor, but the sick. I have not come to call the righteous, but sinners."

Jesus
quoted in Mark 2:17

8

Needy People

It unsettles me somewhat to tell you this story. Why? Because as my children with a twinkle in the eye remind me, I'm old! Want some evidence?

It was Christmas morning in midtown Toronto where a middle-class family named Carter lived. A freckle-faced skinny shy kid by the name of Gary snuck downstairs just as the rest of the household—parents and four teens and twenties siblings—were starting to get up. I was excited by two images. The first was my sister's long stocking hanging by the chimney with care had my name on it. I can't remember what it was full of. No, just for the record, not a lump of coal. But I do remember that in the toe of this long stocking there were always two really, really important things. I got these every year. I didn't get them at any other time—an orange and an apple. Now there was a treat! We weren't poor either.

The other thing that excited me was that I saw for the first time my new britches. Not many others wore these togs but I suppose my mother found them quite durable. You see, I only had one pair of pants every year. And the new ones were the next size up! These were sort of like riding pants but made with heavy brown tweed material, a warm flannel lining and leather patches on the knees. I probably got a toy or two as well. But I don't remember. I was always thrilled to get my new britches. That was my family in the fifties but as I tell the story I feel like my name should have been Engels or Walton—for those who do remember those TV shows. (See you are getting older too!)

I want to stress that we were not under privileged in any way. That was normal middle-class life.

How did we get from that world to this world? If you're not wearing the correct label on your clothes you just won't make it into some groups. I suppose that is all predictable with the world in general. They say the clothes make the man. I don't subscribe to that theory but in a modest way I accommodate it—begrudgingly. I have more important things to do with money than worry about having the perfect attire.

In my view, there's something terribly wrong with such class consciousness when it comes to rolling out the *"good news."* (Mark 1:15) When we can't look people in the eyes and pay attention to the persons instead of the packaging, isn't there something wrong? Hanging out with the right crowd based on exteriors is certainly not something endorsed by Jesus.

When Jesus was having dinner with the wrong people, according to the establishment's scrutinizers, he got an earful. In fact, it was a wealthy crowd which was known for its dysfunctional behavior. When asked about it, this was Jesus' response, *"It is not the healthy who need a doctor, but the sick. I have not come to call the righteous, but sinners."* (Mark 2:17) Oops! Did Jesus actually talk about sinners? That's not politically correct. Who cares? Jesus was into telling the truth and sinners they were. The scrutinizers called them sinners. Jesus admitted they were sinners. And apparently by the statement Jesus makes, it is pretty clear that the people themselves didn't object to being called sinners.

You do get Jesus' point, don't you? Sick people go to doctors. Sinners get called by Jesus. If you get hung up on the word *"sinners"* (Mark 2:17) then Jesus hangs up on you.

There is no doubt that Jesus found tremendous value in meeting with these despised people. It is a mistake to assume the worth and potential of an individual is diminished by the fact they are a sinner. In fact, it is sinners who know they are sinners but who also want their sin problem properly handled who get the special attention of Jesus. There is no implication here that Jesus was about to let anybody stay marinating in their sin and wear a T-shirt with his name on it. Sick people go to doctors to get a prescription for wellness not a validation of their sickness. Jesus calls sinners who are sick and tired of their sin and want a new life.

Earlier in the chapter Jesus said to a paralyzed man while he was still paralyzed, *"Son, your sins are forgiven."* (Mark 2:5) This bugged those establishment police and quite correctly they mumbled to each other, "Who can forgive sins but God alone?" (Mark 2:7) Jesus' statement of response is quite instructive. *"Why are you thinking these things? Which is easier: to say to the paralytic, 'Your sins are forgiven, or to say, 'Get up, take up your mat and walk'? But that you may know that the Son of Man has the authority on earth to forgive sins ..."* he said to the paralytic, *"I tell you, get up, take your mat, and go home."* (Mark 2: 9-11) That is just what happened.

We have skipped over several incidents from Mark's Gospel and the other Gospel writers fill in other incidents and facts in the chronology of Jesus' life. But you should know this is the first place in Mark's Gospel where he introduces the subject of sin. We are only in chapter 2 of 16 chapters. So we are getting to this rather early. It is an important subject. It was then. It is now.

Some have suggested that Jesus never claimed he was God. Excuse me. He just claimed that he had the authority which only God possesses to forgive sins. Then he backed it up with a miracle. Not some psychosomatic effect, an honest to goodness miracle. Sort of looks like an in-your-face, God statement doesn't it?

This guy had been desperate. He had four buddies who ripped a roof off to drop him in front of Jesus' face. This was not a sore back problem. It was a legs don't work problem. And by the way, it was when Jesus saw the put-your-hands-to-work faith of these four friends it was the stimulus for his, *"Son, your sins are forgiven."* (Mark 2:5) statement. Isn't that a beautiful picture? Frankly, there aren't many people with that many friends who would get that innovative and intensive to find a solution. That was some intervention. That is real friendship. We don't know much about these four men. We just know they came to the right place at the right time with the right person and with the right response in their hearts.

What do you suppose their response was when Jesus did the forgiveness part? On first thought you might suggest they groaned. I doubt it. I think they knew they got the best part first for their friend. Remember they already had belief. They already knew the wonders of forgiveness of their own sinfulness because they had believed. And as we discussed earlier, you don't get to believe without repenting. They had already had their turn around. They were desperate to get their lame friend turned around—on the mat or off the mat. I don't think it mattered to them. Now I can't prove that because the text doesn't say it, but is that not a reasonable interpretation?

The key issue this story uncovers is the need for forgiveness. Forgiveness from a person relieves the burden of one's heart concerning a particular issue. Forgiveness from God relieves the burden for eternity! We all need that.

Would it be fair to extend the application of those events to this? Whatever marginalized group you are in now, there is a new possibility for you. The labels don't matter. In fact, it would appear that Jesus shows a special fondness for the underdog. You may have known that before. That is a characteristic of Jesus that does get some air time today. But what is it he wants to do for the underdog? Get the sin problem taken care of. If you haven't done so already you have to take care of your greatest need. You too have a sin problem. We all do.

You can't get that fixed by slapping a set of rules over it like a fresh coat of paint on a rusty car. That old rust will be back. You can't get the sin problem taken care of with a new set of disciplines like going to the health club and losing weight. Your sin problem is permanent as long as you are here on earth. But you can put a serious hurt on it once you experience the forgiveness of Jesus. You can send that sin problem to the penalty box with a game misconduct. If you haven't experienced it, you probably think there is nothing that can take your stinking desires and put them in their place. You will be amazed what the forgiveness of Jesus can do! Jesus is still calling sinners to repentance and belief. Are you listening?

*"He who has ears
to hear,
let him hear."*

*Jesus
quoted in Mark 4:9*

9

It's a Secret!

Kids love it. Adults love it. When someone says, "Let me tell you a secret" it is stimulating. I suppose it makes you feel important. You are about to be placed on the inside track. Not everybody knows this but in a moment you will be one who does.

Have you noticed how many books have the word secret in their titles? I suppose one of the secrets to selling a lot of books is to put the word "secret" in the title. It's a good hook.

Jesus once told his disciples that they had been given, *"The secret of the kingdom of God."* (Mark 4:12) So far in this book we have picked a word, phrase or sentence for the subject of a chapter. Now we're going to take on a whole story. But you will benefit greatly by finding a Bible and reading the story for yourself. Put this book down now and read Mark 4:1 to 20 or the rest of this chapter won't make sense to you.

Jesus used a whole lot of stories or parables. A parable is just a story using everyday items to make one big point. Well at least they were everyday items in the first century context. Most of the time Jesus didn't bother to explain the meaning to people. Most of the people responded by saying in effect, "Nice story but I don't get it." That was okay with Jesus. Jesus would say, *"He who has ears to hear, let him hear."* (Mark 4:9) It was no surprise to Jesus that most people could hear the words with their physical ears but they had earplugs on for their internal ears. One of the things that gets me today is that some people say, "Duh! If this message was so good everybody would buy into it. Since everybody's not buying it obviously it isn't that good. So I'm not going to give it the time of day." I can't even get far enough with them to get them to realize that it was always this way. Jesus himself didn't get anywhere near a hundred percent response.

In this case, Jesus breaks it down for us and gives the precise interpretation of his story. This not only helps those with the story in focus but it gives us some clues how to understand the other stories. By the way, any time Jesus uses a parable he is talking about spiritual truth and this kingdom of God. He is not putting together material for some marketing company to plagiarize. I suppose it is okay to find some secondary applications of his stories but first and foremost get the message he is trying to convey. Get the earplugs out of your internal ears!

Often this particular story is given the title, "The Parable of The Sower." Bad title—not part of Mark's text. There is nothing interesting in the sower here. This is, "The Parable of The Soils." It is the soil that makes this story interesting. The sower uses the same sowing activity and presumably the same amount of seed on all of the soils. But the soils respond differently. And three of four of the soils just don't get it.

Soil #1: Pathway Soil. (Mark 4:4, 15) The seed sits up on top of the trodden down earth and the birds come and get it. Nothing grows. As Jesus points out, we are not talking about actual seed; we are talking about the "word." What word? Well clearly this is the, The-time-has-come.-The-kingdom-of-God-is-near.-Repent-and-believe-the-good-news word. It should never be a shock that some people don't get it. But it might be a shock to hear the reasons why they don't get it. According to Jesus, Satan grabs it. I expect these Pathway Soil people think they have applied their own faculties to this cockamamie message and surfed on by because they came to a studied but quick judgment on it using their own brain. Nope. It was Satan. What an attack that is on their intellectual dignity. Don't you dislike it when someone else makes a decision for you? I sure do! And I don't think you want any Satan character coming along and messing with your opportunity. But it happens all the time to people.

Soil #2: Rocky Soil. (Mark 4:5-6, 16-17) The soil in question here is a flat rock with a very thin layer of topsoil on top of it. To the naked eye one might not even be aware there is a pending problem. After all there is soil here. It just isn't very deep. The people represented here get happy fast. But as soon as they find out that following Jesus isn't a walk in the park, they disappear. It still amazes me that no matter how hard I try to give these people the realistic disclaimers about some of the trouble they will face in following Jesus, they still stay happy and fade away quickly. It is rather like talking to some teenager who has fallen in love and trying to explain to them why the love of their life is not good for them. They know better. And the ironic part is once there is a blow up, they are just as likely to come back and tell you that you never told them. Rocky Soil people can lick your ice cream right under your nose. They seem so responsive and friendly. They nod their heads approvingly of everything you say. Just when you think you have got them on a track and turn your head, "slurp!" your tasty ice cream is gone and so are they.

Soil #3: Thorny Soil. (Mark 4:7, 18-19) The seed takes and it starts to grow. So far; so good. But along comes some pesky weeds. When they grow up they choke the life of the good plants. If Jesus hadn't helped us out here I never could have suggested his inspired interpretation of the situation. But do I ever love it. This is great preaching material! What are these thorns? There are two kinds. #1 the worries of this life. And #2 the deceitfulness of wealth and the desire for other things. Oh man! Tie me down or I might just get carried away here. There is so much to say about the worries of life. I'm just going to make one point as I show exceptional discipline (*SMILE*). This is not a new concept. The worries in your life are not new. It you let them choke off the seed you are making a big mistake. And now for the second concept. Even greater discipline required. Money is sneaky. It ain't gonna get it done for you. More material goods are not what you need. More toys won't fill you up. More investments won't satisfy you. If you put money on your personal throne, all it is going to do for you is whet your appetite for more money. If you don't have a good fix on money, you are headed for the eternal scrap heap. That doesn't mean you can't have money. It does mean that money makes the worst of masters even though it makes a very fine servant. If you don't put the Master (Jesus) over money you're bound to have money master you.

Soil #4: Good Soil. (Mark 4:8, 28) Finally we get to the good soil. Frankly, those first three wear me out because I see so much of them. But I live for a little bit of Good Soil. It's out there. I have found lots of it. I have learned that you have to scatter seed further and faster. When you do, you find more Good Soil. These Good Soil people produce a crop. Some of them 30 times what was sown. That is a great investment. Put down one seed in the right place and get thirty back in the harvest. But since the Good Soil is hard to find and identify it means you have to put four seeds down to get thirty back. And yes, it does take some time for plants to grow fruit. But it is still a great investment! And that is as bad as it gets. It goes up from there to sixty and even one hundred times!

What a great story with a truckload of takeaways! I wish you and I could sit down in our local coffee shop and chat about this for a while. You do realize that there is no room for a fifth kind of soil. Jesus has covered it all. You are in there. Well, actually let me take that back. There is a fifth kind of soil. It is the soil on which no seed has been sown. But since you have now heard the *"good news"* of *"repent and believe"* to receive *"the kingdom of God"* (Mark 1:15) that could no longer be you.

I don't think there is any evidence to suggest that if you are #1, #2 or #3 that, in fact, it is a permanent condition. It may just be a season you are in. What will it take to get you to #4? Isn't that the most important question for the hour? It is up to you. You do have a choice to change. Often people only make such a change when they are under extreme pressure and they don't know where else to turn. But it is entirely possible and within your grasp to wrestle the internal you and make a change. You have to take charge. I promise you, if you will consistently expose yourself to the amazing power within these records of the life of Jesus (Matthew, Mark, Luke and John) you won't even have to think about making that change; it will happen automatically. If you saturate your mind with the *"good news"* (Mark 1:15) you will get it. Are you beginning to grasp this *"good news"*? Here it is in brief. Change your mind, heart and will to point to Jesus and *"the kingdom of God"* (Mark 1:15) and you are in. It's free. It's easy. But you no longer drive the bus. He gets the wheel. And he takes you on a magnificent journey culminating in the perfection of *"the kingdom of God."* (Mark 1:15)

What is the worst thing that can happen if you do saturate your mind with this message? You will at least become an expert on the life of Jesus. That can't be all bad. Some have spent so much time watching reruns of a particular sit com cartoon that he can virtually quote the script from top to bottom of every episode. What a waste. They could have saturated their lives with the eternal Word and they would be much better off today. But they are not reading this book right now and you are. I certainly hope you don't snap back and let yourself be or stay at #1, #2 or #3.

Now you are in on the secret! *"... hear the word, accept it, and produce a crop ..."* (Mark 4:20) It is that simple. Do it and you are in. Don't do it and you forfeit your opportunity. It's time to move on to productivity. #4 here we come!

---

*"This is what
the kingdom of God
is like."*

*Jesus
quoted in Mark 4:26*

10

Story Telling

Everybody loves a story. Over the last century people have become incredibly adept at developing means to get stories to the masses. Printing presses are better and faster. Various forms of media recording have reached a quality level that makes us believe it can't get any better.

Stories create pictures in our minds. Memory experts tell us that our mind files things best in pictures. The theory says that everything we have once heard or seen is in there but sometimes we can't get at it. It is rather like somebody has come in and ransacked our office and taken every single file folder and piece of paper out of the filing cabinets and thrown them all over the floor. It's all in there; we just can't find it anymore.

Have you ever had the experience of watching a movie and about five minutes into it you start to recall the plot line and the characters and exclaimed, "I've seen this before!" I don't like to admit it. It happens to me. I don't remember the title. But the story sticks.

We already got the fact I am old out of the way. How old? Well, I grew up at the end of the radio era just as television was breaking on the scene. There was only one television on our block. I used to like listening to radio drama. I remember lying on the floor listening to the Lone Ranger and his faithful friend, Tonto. I had my own mental version of what that masked man looked like, his white horse and silver bullets. I can still see those tassels on Tonto's leather coat. I don't imagine anybody else's Lone Ranger looked quite like mine. I had to imagine all the visual material.

Listening to stories as opposed to watching stories has its own mystique. I have noticed that our grandchildren would rather have Grandma read them a story than watch one on a video. I don't think it is only the sound of a loving voice. I believe it is also tied to the enjoyment that comes from using the imagination.

Someone has calculated that seventy-five percent of the Bible is in story form. I can't verify the percentage but I know that is the correct neighborhood.

Jesus was a great storyteller. He was fond of telling us about the kingdom of God by using a story or a parable. Now don't go all freaky on me. A parable is not some mystical code with deep meaning hidden under the surface. People love hidden secret meanings that only the apparently enlightened can see. Jesus never gave us any of that sort of thing. He always put the cookies on the bottom shelf, or at least within reach of everyone who cared to reach for them. There are no secret stairways and passwords. Jesus didn't make this hard to figure out. Don't treat it like there is something just beyond your consciousness that you need a sort of trancelike or altered state to grasp. You just need your normal conscious faculties here. Some reject taking a look at Jesus' message because they assume you have to try to create the correct mood or emotional state.

"The kingdom of God" (Mark 1:15) is the realm in which God calls the shots. It starts here in time and flows into the next life. Now, I haven't proven that from the words of Jesus but if we had the space I could. But I am confident that you see that as a plausible possible meaning of his words from what we have covered so far. As we go along I think that will become clearer as well. But, even at that, there is so much more that could be studied. We aren't covering everything Jesus said as recorded by Mark let alone as recorded by Matthew, Luke and John. When he tells us these stories it gives us a clear picture of what to expect both for time and eternity. Many of the parables teach us that

"the kingdom of God" (Mark 1:15) gets very little traction with the many. Inevitably people who start working with the concept of spreading *"the kingdom of God"* (Mark 1:15) underestimate how hard it is to get started and equally they underestimate the amazing potential as the message takes root. This shouldn't be a surprise but it usually is. If you study Jesus' parables you learn an amazing amount about the pattern. Nothing has changed in this wired-up age compared to the word-of-mouth age in which Jesus lived.

We already covered one parable, "The Parable of The Soils." Two more parables are in the same chapter. Let's take a quick look at them from Mark 4. Both of these parables use the concept of *"seed"* (Mark 4:3) once again.

Here is the first one. *"This is what the kingdom of God is like. A man scatters seed on the ground. Night and day, whether he sleeps or gets up, the seed sprouts and grows, though he does not know how. All by itself the soil produces grain—first the stock, then the head, then the full kernel in the head. As soon as the grain is ripe, he puts the sickle to it, because the harvest has come."* (Mark 4:26-29) That's it. It is a simple straightforward story.

Mark doesn't give us any interpretation of the meaning of this story. But later in the chapter we learn this from him. "With many similar parables Jesus spoke the word to them, as much as they could understand. He did not say anything to them without using a parable. But when he was alone with his own disciples, he explained everything." (Mark 4:33-34) The public got the story. But only the committed insiders got the discussion and interpretation. The only parable in the New Testament to which Jesus' explanation is attached is the one in the previous chapter. For all the others we are left on our own.

I think this one is pretty straightforward. We already know that Jesus uses the concept of *"seed"* (Mark 4:3) to refer to his message. This isn't complicated. There are some parts in the hands of the farmer. There are some elements out of his control. The seed doesn't sow itself. The farmer spreads it around. And then the seed grows without him knowing exactly what is going on. He just leaves it alone and lets it sprout and grow. Over time it takes shape. Eventually he gets to take in the harvest.

At this very moment I am creating a seed spreader. I am formulating thoughts in my mind and talking them into a headset. They are showing up on the screen of my notebook computer. I don't actually watch the computer screen. I am looking out the window at some magnificent tall oak trees which are starting to shed their leaves on this early fall day. I am in the Pocanos of Pennsylvania away from home so that I can concentrate. The book that I write in these hours is designed to spread the seed of the kingdom of God. As I imagine the future, I have no ability to comprehend all the detail between these writing moments and your reading moments.

I know what I have to do. I have to write this book. But then it won't do anyone any good if it stays in my computer. I have to take the initiative to turn it into a form that you can read. That is my next step. Somehow it must have traveled from my head to your hand. And chances are we have never met each other. It goes without saying that I cannot control very much about your side of the process. Isn't that just like seed spreading? I will sow the seed of the word and eventually there will be a harvest.

There is always a delay between the time when the seed is spread and when the harvest is taken in. This is not a phenomenon just for our generation. It has always been true. It takes time.

I am just like a farmer. The farmer never knows what kind of crop he will get when he spreads the seed. But under normal circumstances if he sows enough seed at the right time and in the right way he will reap the harvest.

Actually, I am writing this seed spreader because it is my place to do so. My high school English teacher, Elsie Pringle (really—that was her name) would be rolling around in her grave if she ever knew that I had become a writer. I never really passed her course. She just pushed me on to the next grade. Others tell me that I can write. I don't know exactly how that happened. It is just that over time I learned the importance of words. And as time goes by I find myself reducing more and more of those words to forms that can be spread across the world without my personal presence. The older I get the more passionate I become at introducing others to the *"good news."* (Mark 1:15) I just work at spreading it. I leave the results to you and God.

The other parable I want to bring to your attention is this one. *"What shall we say the kingdom of God is like, or what parable shall we use to describe it? It is like a mustard seed, which is the smallest seed you plant in the ground. Yet when planted, it grows and becomes the largest of all garden plants, with such big branches that the birds of the air can perch in its shade."* (Mark 4:30-34) Once again, pretty straightforward.

I don't know a thing about mustard plants. I just know how to get mustard out of the squeeze bottle and on to the hamburger. Apparently, mustard seeds are small. But there is no relationship between the size of the seed and the ultimate size of the mature plant.

Let's try to figure out how that works on the interpretation side. Small start. Big results. See ball. Hit ball.

Maybe the small start is the injection of a first serious thought about the *"good news"* (Mark 1:15) into the mind of one person. Somehow we have to get from there all the way up to this lofty mysterious phrase *"kingdom of God."* (Mark 1:15) Do you remember I suggested that a kingdom is a realm or domain under the control of a king? In this case, the king is God himself. By the way, God is a singular definite being. While we are not given the full exposition by Jesus at this point, it is pretty clear that this isn't some mushy idea where the individual is left to provide the imagination and define a god as whatever he/she wants it to be. The grammar will not allow an understanding of God as an impersonal force. A king is a person. God is a person who takes a personal interest in his kingdom.

As we dig a little deeper, the word *"kingdom"* (Mark 1:15) definitely denotes control. Jesus is describing the realm in which God is in control.

Another Gospel writer, Matthew, is fond of quoting the times Jesus used the term, *"kingdom of Heaven."* (Matthew 4:17) They appear to be interchangeable terms. Now we can extend this concept of the *"kingdom"* (Mark 1:15, Matthew 4:17) beyond the realm of the individual bound by time and on into some glorious future where in the next world God's control is perfectly expressed. Clearly there are real people who go there. And there is not here. That is to say, when people go to the *"kingdom of Heaven"* (Matthew 4:17) they don't just lose their bodies and hang around looking over our shoulders on earth. They go to *"the kingdom of Heaven."* (Matthew 4:17) And further, by the way, it is a place where people get to do what God wants. The ultimate *"kingdom of God"* (Mark 1:15) is not a place where disembodied people get a no hassle vacation sitting on a cloud doing their own thing. And you do remember that Jesus teaches that only those who *"repent and believe the good news"* (Mark 1:15) experience it? Small seed. Big plant.

It goes without saying that I cannot read your mind. I can only imagine the size of the seed or sprout out of the seed that is growing inside of you.

Kingdom seeds are identifiable by a number of characteristics from my perspective. One characteristic of a kingdom seed in a person's mind is a strange emerging desire to look into the *"good news."* (Mark 1:15) I have found that this desire is unsettling and even embarrassing to some. They promised themselves at some point in the past that they would never treat their life or this universe as if religion had any part to play. This conclusion is sometimes drawn because one human being, or even a group of people, imperfectly linked things up in a manipulative or even abusive fashion. "If that's Christianity I want no part of it." Hold on. Neither do I, if they did a bad job. But don't take it from me. Take it straight from Jesus. Just because Jesus has had some terrible salespeople down through the years doesn't mean that his *"good news"* (Mark 1:15) product isn't worth a second look. But please get it from the manufacturer. You don't want some imitation knock off.

Another characteristic of a kingdom seed in a person's heart is the desire to have what people who have it have. For many this is an indescribable characteristic. They just can't quite put their finger on it. There is something attractive about the people who are committed to the kingdom. Even when the kingdom characteristics are all boxed in by a set of old fashioned styles, perspectives and rituals this "thing" bursts out between the cracks.

When you discover that you want it but don't have it and see some people who do have it, spend time with them to figure it out. You need to be with those kind of people in a group to check out how they treat each other. I could leave you to figure this out on your own but I won't. Mark didn't give us the exposition on this one; John did. John records that Jesus said, *"By this all men will know that you are my disciples, if you love one another."* (John 13:35)

Did you catch that? This is about love. That thing is love. You want to be with people who have love. And you can figure out if people are truly Jesus' disciples if they love each other. It will be true that you sense they love you but that is not the point. You need to get on the inside track and observe how they treat each other. Is there a fundamental difference in the bonding of these people that forces you to the conclusion that they would sacrifice for each other? This isn't about group hugs or the number of warm fuzzy comments people make. It is about their behavior in good times and bad. Do you see their support for each other? If you do, place your order for some! By now you should know that means you need to *"repent and believe the good news."* (Mark 1:15)

Well that's all we're going to cover on parables. See ball. Hit ball. Simple story. Straightforward meaning. But with profound implications. The two big takeaways for today are these: #1. To be in sync with *"the kingdom of God"* (Mark 1:15) you spread the seeds around and watch something mysterious happen as some of the seeds grow. #2. The starting size doesn't count. It is small but powerful and creates significant results over time.

If you were hoping that Jesus would unveil a simple solution to make the living out of *"the kingdom of God"* (Mark 1:15) on earth more or less automatic, recalibrate your hope. This appears to be true as he takes over the management of the personal life of a new believer. It often takes time before the fruit becomes obvious. It varies with the individual. I know people who have dropped addictions in a heart beat once they commit to following Jesus. But I know many more individuals in which the change that needs to occur starts slower than that. You want to consider Jesus' brand of *"kingdom of God"* (Mark 1:15) not anyone else's. He is telling the truth. Anyone who offers something that jumps from nothing to everything too quickly is either overstating their experience or has severe memory loss about the nature of the path to the ultimate kingdom of God.

It is really important to explain that this change and growth isn't generated by the citizen. It is generated by the king of the realm. Don't imagine for a second that this is some kind of growth you have to generate on your own. When you get into the kingdom, growth happens. You participate but you don't cause the growth. Let me use an analogy. A normal child grows physically if he/she gets proper nutrition, rest and exercise over time. Often the child lives tilted 45 degrees towards tomorrow. Children can't wait until they are old enough to take on the next phase. Growth is not theirs to control. But many of the things that lead to growth are in their control. That is just like *"the kingdom of God."* (Mark 1:15) Once you get in and conduct yourself properly it is normal for you to change and grow. You don't create the growth. You do control some of the conditions that lead to your growth. And the conditions are really rather simple. Anyone can do it if they have ears to hear.

You might have been tempted in the past to evaluate an alleged expression of the kingdom of God—usually called a church—based on its external characteristics. Big building. Cool band. Lots of people. An emotional bias in the room. Careful. God may or may not be at work if the expression meets media hype standards. After all, Jesus did some pretty spectacular things himself. But this isn't about the externals. You aren't interested in religion are you? I'm not. That is something that comes from the outside. I hope you are interested in the spiritual. That is a from the inside to the outside job. That is where the action is. It might be big and make it to the news. It might not. But it will be the best news for you when you get it right.

The thing you want to focus on is what is happening inside of you and your group of followers. If you are passive and don't take responsibility for your personality you won't thrive. If you associate with a group of people who aren't really prepared to follow too closely after Jesus, you will be tempted to settle back in at the middle of the pack. That is a dreary place to live. Quickly your spiritual life will degenerate into meeting a whole lot of obligations that really don't mean very much to you. You will start to drift and wonder why on earth you are doing the religion thing. All it will do for you is soak up your time and your money. What a drag!

You do a lot of thinking. You can't help it. Do you find yourself suspending the hard-work thinking in favor of living in a fantasy world? Perhaps your favorite escape appears innocent enough. And you certainly need an element of rest and recreation in your life. I'm not talking about that. When you get down to those, "I really should get my act together" kinds of thoughts, how do you handle them? What happens when a, "What if there is an afterlife and I'm not ready for it" thought sneaks up on you? What do you do when, upon reflection, you find yourself admitting, "That was a disgusting thing to do?" Do you just glue the cell phone back on your ear and call a friend for no good reason? Do you fire up an Internet based game and get lost in a character you invented? Or perhaps you drown your deeper questions in something chemical to numb your mind. Even natural hormones can be used to numb your mind in illicit ways.

Could it be that some of those engaging deeper ideas are mustard seeds of the kingdom of God? Don't you think you should explore that possibility?

"Take nothing for your journey except..."

*Jesus
quoted in Mark 6:8*

11

First Presentation

How well do you remember the first time you had to give a speech? Did you just screw up your face like I asked you to take a bite of a grapefruit-sized lemon? It isn't the fondest memory for most of us.

For me, as I suspect it was for most, that first speech came in a school classroom. To preserve you the pain of remembering your event let me tell you about mine.

First, it is probably helpful for you to understand that I was quiet and reserved in school. The idea of getting up in front of people was way beyond my comfort zone. The protocol for speech giving, as I recall it, was we were each to prepare a speech on a chosen topic. We were to plan on five minutes. I recall that we were taught how to create notes on cards to help us remember our speech during delivery. We weren't exactly sure of the day on which our speech was to be given. An order was assigned. But there was some uncertainty about which day our individual number would come up. I had estimated that my turn would come on the next day. Wrong. I was called. I stood up. I had my three by five cards in hand. My mind sat right back down again. Seriously, I had nothing to say. Some evil little gremlin jumped inside my internal hard drive and deleted or jumbled all the files. I guess I must have uttered some semi-intelligent sounds. Two minutes later my body went to join my mind at my desk. I recall looking at the teacher for some hopeful comment. She stretched a bit and found something nice to say. I appreciated the fact that she didn't tell the whole truth and humiliate me in front of my peers. I made a note to myself that day to find a desk job when I grew up.

I will spare you the details of my further humiliating public speaking events. Trust me. That wasn't my only strike out.

Any important skill starts somewhere. It wouldn't be a skill if you didn't have to learn it. Over time things improve. But you have to start somewhere. There is a first time for everything, you know. And I could load up this paragraph with some other trite sayings you already know.

It was the same deal for the disciples. As Mark unfolds the story for us we are in Mark 6 when Jesus, in effect, says, "Now it is your turn." We skipped over a wonderful little snippet from chapter 3. Here it is. "Jesus went up on a mountainside and called to him those he wanted, and they came to him. He appointed twelve—designating them apostles—that they might be with him and that he might send them out to preach and to have the authority to drive out demons." (Mark 3:13-15) Now in chapter 6 it is game time for these twelve.

But first, notice what Jesus had in mind for these twelve. Jesus called them because he wanted them. The entrance requirements were not expressed. But their readiness to join in was clear because they came to him. There are three classes in the curriculum here. The first and most important was Jesus wanted them to be with him. Others followed him around—even thousands on occasion. But these twelve were the ones who were going to live with Jesus. He invited them to develop an insider's viewpoint. But it was very clear from the outset that he intended to send them out to preach and to have authority to drive out demons.

Just on a side note, we are only touching on the miraculous element of Jesus' ministry in this book because we are focusing on his words. Suffice it to say that the primary purpose of the miracles he performed was to authenticate his God-given authority. There were four time periods in the Bible when God used the tool of miraculous intervention. That was not his general method of operation over the period of Bible history. He used this mechanism only at the times of inauguration of a new spiritual economy. It was the way God chose to work through the times of the life of Jesus and on some occasions during the establishment of the church in its early phases. This was a time of new beginnings. There is no Biblical or historical evidence to indicate that we ought to expect God to use miracles in a consistent pattern at all times and in all places.

Now let's get back to our story and the words of Jesus. We are in Mark 6. Jesus calls the twelve to him and sends them out in pairs. So there are six two-person mission teams. This is designed by Jesus as their first short-term mission experience. School is out for now. It is time for a field trip to put it into practice.

Jesus' instructions here are interesting. He says, *"Take nothing for your journey except ... "* (Mark 6:8) He named a few essential items and a few nonessential items. Clearly, Jesus didn't want them to get messed up with a lot of baggage. The nonessential items are astounding. No food. No suitcase. No money. The essential items were a staff and sandals. All they needed was the bare necessities to get them there on foot. Don't fill up the SUV. Just get going. Later on Jesus relaxed these conditions a bit but the attitude was still the same. I doubt that there was a swoosh logo on the back of their T-shirts. But ringing in their ears there had to be the equivalent of, "Just do it!"

Don't sample all the accommodation possibilities in a town. Only go where they get it. If they don't welcome you or listen to you shake the dust off your feet. Shake it or you won't make it.

Over the years I have watched a lot of hand wringing from people in churches. They would be happy to put up a billboard if it didn't cost so much. They would be happy to put literature into every home as long as they buy a distribution service rather than do it themselves. And they certainly can't afford the postage. And nobody reads that kind of literature anyway. And that method of talking to people is invasive. And nobody likes junk mail. And they would do radio advertising but they can't afford that either. And they can just put an ad on the church page because that's cheaper than advertising on the other pages. When I suggest they might like to just use their voice and talk to people, I get a whole new set of excuses. "But I don't have anybody to talk to." "My neighbors aren't interested." "I don't like talking to strangers." "I'm too busy." "They know where to find us."

Wow! How did we get from the "just bang on another door until somebody welcomes you, listens to you and feeds you until it's time to go" attitude to a "catch me if you want to" attitude. It is a terribly long way from the instructions of Jesus which put the initiative into the hands of a pair of semi-trained, weak-kneed fishermen to where many people are today.

Jesus is on record here. Time for hot brass tacks. Get up. Get ready. Get going. Get it done. Get over it. Get to the next door. This is what you can expect on the inside of a group of people who are tracking with him. And you can be quite clear that when you get into his training program there will come a day when you too will need to get uncomfortable and talk to some strangers on his behalf.

That whole concept of you becoming some raving evangelist is probably as scary a thought as you have ever had. Well first of all, it is not anywhere near as bad as your worst fears. And nobody wants you to become an overzealous jerk. But it certainly wouldn't be fair to let you live with an illusion that there isn't a proactive role for you to take in due time.

I expect that you know some people who will tell you that they follow Jesus. And I wouldn't presume to know how to evaluate their sincerity without knowing their whole story. But I can tell you this. If you stick this chapter, or for that matter, this entire book under their nose and ask for their opinion as to whether this fairly captures the heart of Jesus' teaching you will learn something. You might learn that they agree and are yearning to live it out. You might learn that they disagree entirely. In either case, conduct your following dialogue in front of their open Bible to make sure they can explain their position. The very exercise of this kind of discussion might be just what you need to fill in some of the blanks and get you started on a wonderful adventure, with Jesus and your friend or with Jesus and without your friend. You see, it is the same thing today; you have to shake it or you won't make it!

"...it is what comes out of a man that makes him 'unclean.'"

*Jesus
quoted in Mark 7:16*

12

Matters of the Heart

Psychology 101 was a great disappointment for me. I thought it was going to help me understand much more about what makes people tick. I never knew that it was going to contain so much information about Pavlov's dogs and lab mice. It is not that I didn't learn. I did. I just expected to come away with many more "ah hah" moments.

Over the years I have had so many people wistfully say to me, "I think I need to take a psychology course so that I can understand my spouse/teenager/boss." I try not to be too brutal as I tell them that would be way too little and way too late to solve their problem. Besides if they were to pick up ten textbooks from ten different theorists and study them they would be likely to identify dozens of conflicting opinions amongst them. That would be like loading each arm up with five wristwatches each pointing to a different time. That will not provide much precision in time keeping.

There really is a better idea. You can learn everything it is essential to know by studying the words of Jesus. I am not saying you can learn everything. But you can make a correct start.

We are not working in the Gospel of John for this book but I highly recommend it to you. In that Gospel John asserts that Jesus was on hand at the beginning of time and was God himself. John, one of Jesus' three closest friends, further explains that, *"Through him all things were made; without him nothing was made that has been made."* (John 1:3) It is possible that the voltage in that is way too high for you at the moment but you can check it out for yourself. Study the logic of John 1:1-17 and you cannot draw any other conclusion. If in fact, as I'm quite certain, Jesus created people, his opinion on what makes us tick has got to be worth more than any twenty-seven Ph.D.s crammed into a phone booth.

So let's delve into that possibility. Here we go. *"Listen to me, everyone, and understand this. Nothing outside a man can make him 'unclean' by going into him. Rather, it is what comes out of a man that makes him 'unclean.'"* (Mark 7:14-15) His Jewish audience was perpetually concerned about getting the correct formula. Jerusalem was the center of Jewish worship. There were more religious rituals and protocols than you could ever imagine. People were required to go through certain ceremonial washings and eat certain things in the correct order and at the right time. There was a great fear that if they didn't get it correct they would not be accepted by God and would face dire consequences. Jesus is teaching that it is not the stuff from the outside but the stuff from the inside that is going to mess you up.

It is commonly believed by some that Christianity is about learning a new set of rules and traditions. They mistakenly believe that the whole point of Christianity is to get people to conform to certain meetings, dress codes and behaviors. They miss the mark by quite some distance. This is entirely a matter of the heart first of all. The rest should follow naturally but only as driven by the heart.

The disciples didn't get it. This inside-out concept was way beyond them. So Mark continues with the story. Jesus gave them some very important information which obviously by his comment, as you will read in a moment, seemed pretty elementary.

"Are you so dull?" he asked. *"Don't you see that nothing that enters a man from the outside can make him unclean? For it doesn't go into his heart but into his stomach and then out of his body. What comes out of the man is what makes him 'unclean.' For from*

within, out of men's hearts come evil thoughts, sexual immorality, theft, murder, adultery, greed, malice, deceit, envy, slander, arrogance and folly. All these evils come from inside and make a man 'unclean.'" (Mark 7:18-23)

As I fill in the body language in the imaginary pictures in my head I see Jesus starting off by rolling his eyes and then blasting out this illustrative list of evils that come from inside of people. He isn't naming all of the possible sins. I think he's just slapping out a long list to hammer away at their dull hearts. If I may paraphrase it, he is saying, "Don't you get it! People suck. They are full of garbage!" No amount of ritual is going to fix that big of a problem.

I am going to repeat that because it seems to me to be attacking a lot of what I hear. No amount of ritual is going to fix that big of a problem. We have a problem. Jesus was adamant about this. We come back to that "S" word people don't like. Sinner. We are all sinners. If you don't get that you're just like the disciples. Brace yourself for this. This is not me talking. This is Jesus. You are dull. It is not that we all do all bad all the time. But it is that we are capable of that sort of garbage at any moment. We are all born as ticking time bombs loaded up with a sin nature.

As I peruse the bookshelves in the religious and the psychology sections of bookstores I find far more books that deny the central problem than I do those that admit it and offer solutions for it. The current material on the shelves is not much different than other material that has been around for a very long time. It tends to say that if you peel the onion of your personality and get down deep enough you are going to find God. According to Jesus that is nonsense, is it not? This idea is very offensive to many who have been led to believe that at their core they are good.

Imagine for a moment that I am a medical doctor and I have discovered that you have terminal cancer. What would you rather I do? When you come for your appointment I could probably tell you that you are just going through a phase with some temporary discomfort and we can medicate it to minimize your pain. Or I could tell you the truth. Actually, some people would opt for the first alternative since they are going to die no matter what. But now let me add another dimension. Pretend science has just found a solution for the particular kind of cancer that you have. It has been one hundred percent terminal up until now. But as of this last month, with scientific certainty, we have a pill for it that will remove all cancer from your system. Now what would you like me to say? "I feel your pain. Take two aspirin and get a good night's sleep and I'm sure you'll feel better in the morning." Hardly. In my imaginary analogy the cancer is sin and the pill is the *"good news"* (Mark 1:15) according to Jesus. This isn't a new solution. However, it is the one solution that is often ignored because some don't think they will like the taste of the "pill." Does it make sense to take your cues from those who have never truly tasted or from those who have? I have. Honest. You don't need to screw up your face and hold your nose. This is really, really good news!

It is no big loss to find out that you are a sinner if you at the same time find out there is a solution and that the solution is delicious!

In this particular incident Jesus does not go on to explain his role in the universe as the solution for the sin problem. But when you take the weight of his entire oral ministry, it is quite clear that he knew he was and was careful to explain that to people. As we understand Jesus' view of people and the urgency of the situation, it gets much easier for us to understand the urgency in his voice when he said, *"Repent and believe the good news."* (Mark 1:15)

Quite frankly, the next new handsome smooth voiced theorist/practitioner will break on the scene. There is a high degree of probability that this new guru will flip around a few old words in a cute new way. Since twelve is a pretty tedious number and seven has been overworked, I would like to guess the new program is going to have fewer steps or key points for you. But if the new system doesn't address this fundamental problem of the heart it will fail. It may sell a lot of information; it may get a lot of airtime on the talk show circuit but it won't solve many problems. You know what? We have a two step program here and it really works. What are those two steps? Repent. Believe.

We are getting back to fundamentals again. Remember old Charlie Hustle? See ball. Hit ball. I am a sinner. I needed a Savior. He found me! How about you?

> *"Who do people say
> I am?"*
>
> — *Jesus*
> *quoted in Mark 8:27*

13

What's His Name

My mother never had a middle name. Middle names always seemed like a waste to me. As a curious child I asked my mother what they were for. I don't remember asking my parents a lot of tough questions like that. But I suppose I did. I must have taxed them to the limit. I was their fifth child and by the time I came along they probably were just a little tired of answering that kind of question. But I digress. In this case, my mother had an interesting answer. I don't think she really had any idea about what middle names were for but she did know that growing up without one was a lot harder to explain than having one.

Perhaps so. But then when you give your child a middle name like Verdun (pronounced VER-dun) you swing the pendulum in another direction. I know. That is my middle name. I can't imagine that not having a middle name is any more difficult to explain than having a middle name like that.

I didn't appreciate it as a child. I do now. That was the name of my Uncle Bert. He didn't like the name Verdun so he chose to go by Bert. Verdun (Bert) was a soldier who gave his life in Italy at the end of World War II shortly before I was born. My mother (Phyllis) was the oldest of six children and Bert was the youngest. My older sister tells me of her memory of the tremendous shock my mother felt at the time Bert was killed. In some small way Phyllis' little baby Gary—her youngest—carrying her little brother's name must have been a comfort to her. As an adult, I consider it a privilege to have a distinct middle name like Verdun.

Naming conventions change from culture to culture. But they always carry some significance. Today in the West we tend to give less significance to the names we choose for our children than at other times and places. But we can't get away from it; our names still have meaning at some level. We like to hear our name. And it strengthens our relationship to others when we use their name in conversation.

When you spend a lot of time with people you get around to discussing all sorts of interesting topics such as names. Imagine taking a 30 mile hike with a dozen other people. As you walk along you would walk in smaller clusters of perhaps two to four people. Individuals would naturally rotate in and out of these groups over time. Sometimes it would be the subject matter of conversation that would draw people in and out of the clusters. Once in awhile an individual would raise their voice to communicate something for the ears of the entire group. It would have been no different in Jesus' day.

During one of these long days Jesus had a discussion with the twelve about names and identities. He asked this question, *"Who do people say I am?"* (Mark 7:27) If you are on a hike with a dozen others I wouldn't recommend you pipe up and ask that question of a group. Once they get over their initial shock of where that question is coming from their sense of humor is likely to kick into gear. It might start with, "They say you're the guy that starts conversations with weird questions" and go downhill from there. But the question in this case and its context implies an overlay of, "What do people say about me?" That adds a vulnerability and intimacy to the discussion.

I mentioned earlier that with these incidents in Jesus' life we just get an essential outline of the conversation or event. We get all the information we need; but no doubt there was quite an intriguing discussion along that dusty road that day.

Jesus was very good at using instructive questions. The Gospel writers include a lot of dialogue between Jesus and other individuals or groups. As often as not Jesus starts that discussion with a question. Even though, according to his own self awareness, he was the greatest authority in the universe, he made a habit of getting other people involved by asking leading questions to get them thinking. In this case, the answer to the question, *"Who do people say I am?"* (Mark 8:37) might add some polling information but it really wouldn't change any of the reality. People might be right. Or people might be wrong. Their opinions count only so far as they impact the conclusion drawn by the serious inquirer.

It is still true today. Gathering up a large number of incorrect opinions on truth can never lead one to the truth. People have a hard time grasping this fact. There is some comfort in fraternizing with a herd of people regardless of what direction they are heading. Many individuals caught up in a gang or cult might actually want out of the group because they can see it is headed in the wrong direction but they can't find the exit door easily. In a much milder context, an individual might want out of a discussion or activity being perpetuated by a group of friends but still prefer not to take a stand and walk away from the group.

If at this present time you are associating with a group, set of friends or family who reject taking Jesus straight up, and if you want to follow him, there is going to be a separation price for you to pay. But you might also be surprised to know that others are likely to follow you into a new way of life if you take a stand.

Now let's get back to the disciples. Jesus asks, *"Who do people say I am?"* (Mark 8:37) The answers in reply from the disciples indicate that the public believes Jesus is a serious player. It is natural for people to attempt to link up something that is unknown with something that is known. Sometimes the linkage isn't entirely helpful. "It tastes like chicken" might not be strong enough of an endorsement to get you to eat some animal you have never tasted before.

The range of answers Jesus received from his small group discussion won't mean a lot to you if you don't know the players suggested. So let me give you some background.

All of the suggestions that come forward point to individuals who were known as spiritual leaders. They were all leaders. So we know Jesus had progressed that far with the masses. They saw him as a leader. He was not elected or appointed as the leader by anyone. But clearly, he occupied leadership space in the public consciousness. And the nature of that leadership was something like the prophets of old. It is not so much that he was making statements about the future as he was making bold statements about how to fix this world and how to straighten up the affairs of individual lives.

Humans are incurably spiritual. That is to say, we care to direct our lives towards lofty ideals which transcend the mundane. We are drawn to find meaning and significance. We look for a higher cause. The tragedy is that in our search so many just settle. So many give up and opt for a set of familiar routines deliberately designed to postpone the big questions. So many entertain themselves with inconsequential affairs and toys. So many find something to medicate their internal yearning down to a semicomatose state. So many others choose an earthly cause which may be good as far as it goes but it cannot stretch into eternity. Pick target. Work like crazy. Get bored. Switch target. Eventually avoid getting involved.

The Jewish populous did not believe in reincarnation. But in trying to find a pigeonhole for Jesus all they could think of was bringing back people from the past. These guys were not inconsequential. John the Baptist who had been assassinated was a fiery preacher who broke on the scene just prior to Jesus. In Mark1:5 it is reported that all Jerusalem took a trip to one of his campaigns. He was the forerunner of Jesus by his own admission. He was the one who pointed to Jesus as the ultimate solution. There were many similarities. Matthew records for us the essence of John the Baptist's message. *"Repent, for the kingdom of Heaven is near."* (Matthew 3:2) John the Baptist immersed people in water as a symbol of their commitment to turning from their sins. John the Baptist was tough. When a group of religious leaders came to check him out, he said to them, *"You brood of vipers! Who warned you to flee from the coming wrath? Produce fruit in keeping with repentance ..."* John (The Gospel writer and close associate of Jesus) quoted John the Baptist. *"When John the Baptist saw Jesus coming toward him he said, 'Look, the Lamb of God, who takes away the sin of the world! This is the one I meant when I said, 'A man who comes after me has surpassed me because he was before me.' I myself did not know him, but the reason I came baptizing with water was that he might be revealed to Israel.'"* (John 1:29-31) Obviously, that segment of the public who thought Jesus was John the Baptist coming back again didn't get the message John the Baptist was trying to get across.

Another name that had been bandied about to summarize Jesus' identity was Elijah. Elijah was a great historical figure to the Jews as recorded in the Jewish scriptures (the Old Testament to Christians). He was the one who, like John the Baptist, inaugurated a brand new beginning which was known as the time of the prophets. That was pretty elite company as well for the public to suggest. It was common then, and it has become common for non Jesus followers down through time, to give Jesus the status of prophet. They too will say they believe in Jesus. Well, they believe Jesus was a religious leader. They believe Jesus was a historical figure. They might even believe that Jesus pointed the way to God. But they certainly do not put their trust in Jesus as the only solution for the sin problem. That is what Jesus meant when he used the word *"believe."* (Mark 1:15)

Public discussion put other names on the ballot. We don't know which names they suggested. Mark just tells us there were people who suggested Jesus was, *"One of the prophets."* (Mark 8:28)

I want you to notice that nobody suggested, "Nice gentle guy who helps people"; "Sincere but misdirected lunatic"; or "Media preacher out to make a buck." All of the suggested answers gave Jesus some level of respect.

And now Jesus, as a great discussion leader, brings it down to the personal. It always comes down to the personal. It might be threatening to have to come to the place where you mark your ballot. But in the end of the day not making a decision is in fact making a decision. Nobody can claim, "I didn't have time to make up my mind."

Jesus asked, *"Who do you say I am?"* (Mark 8:29)

Peter answered, *"You are the Christ."* (Mark 8:29) Bing!

Again that might not mean much. Jesus accepted the term. He didn't use it of himself frequently, but he did use it. The problem was that the term had collected so much baggage. The term "Christ" is the Greek equivalent of the Jewish term "Messiah." The root meaning here is, "The Anointed One." When a king was appointed they poured oil on his head ceremonially to establish his kingship and thus anointed him. So the term here is the rough equivalent of "Ultimate and Perfect King." For the Jews this term had degenerated into one with political and nationalistic overtones. Jesus wasn't about to identify with petty politics and freedom wishes to get out from under Rome so they could mess things up on their own. Jesus' message was timeless and infinitely higher. Short term solutions for time mean something, just not much. Jesus was, and is the solution for eternity.

Matthew describes this event more completely for us. Peter had some other things to say and so did Jesus. But we have quite enough to handle here.

Jesus accepted Peter's answer because it was precisely what he wanted to hear. Peter often served as the spokesperson for the twelve so we can assume all heads nodded as Peter supplied the answer.

You knew I would get to this. So? See ball. Hit ball. What is your basic answer? Who do you say Jesus is? That is not a theoretical question for the other person. It is a very personal question for you. If you agree that Jesus is the only solution, then what changes are you prepared to make to show it? A good start would be a resolute commitment to take what he said and build your life around it. And the only way you are really going to get some traction is to get with a group of others headed in the same direction who can help keep you on track as you too help them. Have you picked your group yet? What is the worst thing that can happen if you give it an honest chance for about a quarter of a year? What is the best thing that can happen if you give it an honest chance? If you can't find a group, contact me and I will find one with you. But chances are you already have one in your vicinity and you know when and how they meet. Get to it!

"If anyone would come after me, he must deny himself and take up his cross and follow me."

Jesus
quoted in Mark 8:34

14

The Price and The Prize

You have heard it said, "No pain. No gain." It is usually applied to physical exercise. I have a problem with getting enough exercise.

One of the things for me is that I dislike doing something that has no end purpose. For example, I mentioned that I am writing this at a place away from home in the serenity and beauty of the Poconos in Pennsylvania. Yesterday I was out for a walk down the mountain road here and passed a gentleman who had just paused to lean on a shovel. He was turning over some ground and planting a few shrubs. We were both breathing heavily. I made some comment about there being no end of work to which he agreed. I kept walking. He kept planting.

When I returned past his house about a half hour later I saw his nicely planted shrubs in front of his well manicured yard and house. I got my exercise for the day but I had nothing to show for it. He has his exercise and a little nicer property. I felt slightly cheated. We both got a little pain. But he got the better gain for his effort.

Life is full of cost and benefit analyses. Is it worth it? We ask that question directly and indirectly every day. Lazy people create a different equation than industrious people. For the lazy person very little is worth an effort. Without an effort little gets accomplished. You can see the difference in a well kept house and a run down house. The person with the run down house would like to have the well kept house but simply isn't willing to pay the price.

What price are you willing to pay to save your life? Physically you would likely go to great ends if your life was threatened. But the following quote of Jesus put the question at a much higher level.

"If anyone would come after me, he must deny himself and take up his cross and follow me. For whoever wants to save his life will lose it, but whoever loses his life for me and for the gospel will save it. What good is it for a man to gain the whole world, yet forfeit his soul? Or what can a man give in exchange for his soul? If anyone is ashamed of me and my words in this adulterous and sinful generation, the Son of Man will be ashamed of him when he comes in his Father's glory with the holy angels." (Mark 8:34-38)

Did you know that there is only one way to save your life? Jesus lays it out for us here. I don't think this is hard to grasp at all. But over the years I have had many who claim to be followers of Jesus find this to be very hard to understand. My conclusion is that they thought the contract with Jesus was far different than what he demanded. Perhaps, they thought the sort of commitment Jesus talks about here was for some spiritual elite. You know the monks, holy men, preachers and the like. Sorry folks. He isn't talking to a special group here.

This isn't any different in essence than what he has said before but it might grab your interest and awareness at a higher level.

First, notice the application is for *"anyone."* No exemptions here. *"If anyone would come after me, ..."* (Mark 8:34) So anyone with a desire to follow Jesus and experience the benefits—and the benefits are huge for both life in the here and in the hereafter—must meet the qualifications.

Qualification #1: Deny Himself. (Mark 8:34) By the way, until this current generation it has been the standard in English literature (as in many languages) to use the masculine pronoun as a generic reference to both males and females. This is a message for all people. Otherwise we have to do some crazy word flips such as him/herself. That is rather awkward. When someone comes up with an easy way to do that I will join the parade. Males and females are both equal and as far as Jesus is concerned using the masculine form covered both. The attention needs to be given to this term *"deny."* Deny what? What do you think Jesus meant when he said, *"Must deny himself"*? Now don't go trying to water it down. You would have to agree that from Jesus' perspective this was doable. So obviously he isn't asking you to commit some form of intellectual suicide or put your faculties in a freezer. I don't think this is hard. He is, among other things, saying, "Give me your PDA, the keys to your car and house, your bank card and your remote control. You are no longer in charge of the agenda for you once you start with me." *"If anyone would …"* Qualification #1 is in essence, "It's my way or the highway." No one could accuse Jesus of not being clear. And nobody could accuse him of not setting the bar high enough. By the way, when you compare Luke's recording of this statement he adds the word *"daily."* (Luke 9:23) So if you think this was just for some initiation week or something, forget it. This is an agenda management every day from this day forward.

I made a commitment to this life as Jesus describes it when I was very young. I had no idea what that would mean as I grew and all of my human faculties emerged to adulthood. And I don't find it hard to admit to you that there have been more days than I care to count when I messed up and struck out on my own path. But I am here to tell you every time I did it was a bad idea and sooner or later I got back to his agenda. I have a better day every single day I give him all my thoughts, feelings and decisions to manage. He is much better at managing my life than I would be. How do I know when he is in charge? Here are a few clues. I study his road map so that I can know the difference between right and wrong. When I become aware that I am off track, I fix it. People tell me when I am off track. I carefully evaluate their input. My own insides tell me when I am off track. Now of course my insides also present a faulty option frequently. I do chase that faulty option far too frequently if I don't get back to reviewing the written road map and my commitment to it.

Qualification #2: Take Up His Cross. (Mark 8:34) I think most people miss the point on this one. They refer to something undesired that comes into their life and resign themselves to its presence. They say, "I guess this is just my cross to bear." And there are some hurts and disappointments that must be borne by all people. Generally, we have far fewer in the West than people do in other parts of the world. But that is not the point. If you didn't go out and voluntarily get the cross, whatever it is, how can it meet the qualification of *"Take up."* If it was imposed you didn't get to take it up.

So if a cross is not a tough burden imposed from the outside, what is it? You can hardly miss making a connection with the cross that Jesus died on. He gave his life willingly and died a despicable death for us as our substitute. *"For even the Son of Man did not come to be served, but to serve, and to give his life as a ransom for many."* (Mark 10:45) It is helpful to realize as you ponder that when Jesus used the word *"cross"* here, he hadn't yet faced his cross. He had just started to introduce the fact that he would be put to death shortly to his disciples. (Mark 8:31) And they were not pleased. The disciples wanted another agenda. But as Jesus was about to take up his own cross it was very clear that he was a man on a mission.

At this point in the life of Jesus he makes his disciples aware that the clock is ticking as he moves toward his death in Jerusalem. And that was not an easy thing, even for the Son of Man. But he was the Son of Man on the Ultimate Mission. That desire to be the perfect representative or as John the Baptist put it, *"Look, the Lamb of God, who takes away the sin of the world!"* (John 1:29) was the essence of his divinity and his humanity. His mission was so very clear.

How could you possibly understand the *"take up his cross"* statement required of every follower to mean anything other than adopting a parallel mission? When one becomes a follower of Jesus the every day price paid is to structure life as a mission to spread the message of the ultimate missionary. God only had one son and he gave him to be a missionary. If you want to go after Jesus there is no other alternative. You too will make it your personal purpose to drive your life into that mission at any and every cost.

But we are not done yet. Take a deep breath. It gets more comforting with the next qualification.

Qualification #3: Follow Me. (Mark 8:34) When life is easy, *"follow me."* When life is hard, *"follow me."* When you can't see your way in the dark, *"follow me."* When everyone around you deserts you, *"follow me."* When your body breaks down into ill health, *"follow me."* When you face death, *"follow me."* When you just get stuck in life, *"follow me."* When you enter a new phase, *"follow me."* When you achieve amazing success in the eyes of others, *"follow me."*

There is no place or circumstance to which that simple directive does not apply. *"Follow me."* If you want to know how to follow him, it's easy. Don't guess at it. See ball. Hit ball. Just pick up the words of Jesus and see which principle he stated would apply in the situation in which you find yourself and do it. Don't get hung up trying to figure out if it feels right. Get over that one. Most of the time if you go with your gut you may go to the gutter. This isn't a system where you look inside for answers. Which part of the phrase, *"follow me"* don't you get? Find out what Jesus said that is relevant to your situation and apply it.

I suspect that some who are looking at this are saying, "You are joking, right? I can't demonstrate that much faith or sacrifice." Okay, it's up to you. You can get the short term gain and take the eternal pain if you like. But why would you? The price of that neglect of your humanity is far too high. We have all known people who have neglected the needs of their body and as a result have died young. On their death bed they sing a far different tune than they did when they were younger and could have done something about it. We look on them with some pity and grief but we are all too aware that they took a payoff early in life and now it is payback time. We might not say it to them or others around but we all know it.

Question: *"What good is it for a man to gain the whole world, yet forfeit his soul?"* (Mark 8:36) Answer: No good anyone has thought of yet. Notice Jesus says there is a soul. Jesus also says that soul can be forfeited. The gain which created the forfeiture was in life here on earth. Even if you have all the palaces in the world to sleep in and all the status and accolades that put you in the lobby at the hall of fame, it is a terrible price to pay. Of course, if Jesus wants your statue in the lobby of some hall of fame he will work that out for you. But if that is your agenda and not his you are worse than out of luck. Forfeit. Game over. No appeals.

The results of rejecting these three qualifications are very clear. *"If anyone is ashamed of me and my words in this adulterous and sinful generation, the Son of Man will be ashamed of him when he comes in his Father's glory with the holy angels."* (Mark 8:38) Jesus is hereby promising to return as The Judge. And the standard as described here is simple. If you are ashamed now you are headed on the fast track to be shunned by him then. You really need to grasp that this is not some hypothetical possibility. Maybe it will happen. Maybe it won't. No. No! This, according to Jesus, is an absolute certainty. Some people are used to messing up and then saying, "But it wasn't my fault." That might get you a second chance on the job or at school. After all, it is difficult for the boss and the principal to know what really happened. But that technique simply will not work. Jesus is coming back. You don't get an appeal of his sentence. The gavel will drop. It will be over. Why on earth would you take the risk that he isn't telling the truth? What evidence can you bring to bear to suggest another end to it all? Oh, yes the one about all the people around you who don't think this is the whole truth. I thought we covered that already. This is not about them. Remember they could be Soils #1, #2, or #3. Do you not wish to be Soil #4?

The offer he makes is really amazing and the after death benefits are out of this world! The decision made in time determines the outcome in eternity.

The Price and The Prize

Life coaching is the hot thing today. You no longer get yourself a therapist. That might imply that you have serious defects. You now go out and get a life coach. That implies you just have a little fine tuning to do. A coach will allegedly get you unstuck. The other consultant you need is a personal trainer to handle all the body and exercise issues. As you can imagine there are good therapists and bad therapists. There are good coaches and bad coaches. And some personal trainers are better than others. So if you were going to find one of these which kind would you want—a good one or a bad one? Duh. What if there were a coach/therapist/trainer in town who was taking on new clients and this coach/therapist/trainer had the reputation as being the best there is and the price was on a sliding scale depending on what you could afford? Would you jump at the opportunity? What if that one was Jesus? He is available. You can afford it. You can't afford not to follow him.

"I tell you the truth, anyone who will not receive the kingdom of God like a little child will never enter it."

Jesus
quoted in Mark 10:15

Kid's Stuff

Children bring a lot of joy into this world. Seemingly, they can always find something to play with or something to do. They don't need fancy contrived entertainment experiences.

Much more than the rest of us they find wonderment in simple things—especially natural things.

I find I have learned a lot about my children since they became adults. They tend to have a different interpretation on their childhood years than I recall. To their memory, things that we always did as a family in actuality may have had only three or four occurrences. But because they were so cherished, as children, they played them over and over again in their minds. I am so pleased that many of their happy memories are connected to the regular pattern of our family to attend church every week. There was no better event for them in both their view and ours (Wendy and me). We never had to deal with the oft repeated, "I had religion crammed down my throat." They knew that life on the private side of our family was aligned with the public side and both were tuned to follow Jesus. They knew that their relationship with Jesus was their own choice and that it made perfectly good logical sense. There wasn't any point in trying to find a better alternative.

It grieves me to watch parents talk one way and live another. Pious words about inculcating good values without matching behavior just plain stinks. One sure way to lose your children is to hypocritically expect standards of them you are not prepared to keep yourself. Another way to drive them from home is to give their perspectives and opinions very little respect. If you add to that a good dose of lip service about following Jesus mixed with an inconsistent commitment to being with his people, you have a perfect recipe for disaster.

I love this event from the life of Jesus. *"People were bringing little children to Jesus to have him touch them, but the disciples rebuked them. When Jesus saw this, he was indignant. He said to them, 'Let the little children come to me, and do not hinder them, for the kingdom of God belongs to such as these. I tell you the truth, anyone who will not receive the kingdom of God like a little child will never enter it.'"* (Mark 10:13-15)

Obviously, Jesus loved children and got rip snorting mad when his disciples thought it an inconvenience to have children take up his time.

But in this wonderful teaching moment Jesus gave us an illustration of an important dimension of human response required to enter *"the kingdom of God."* (Mark 10:13) The first thing to note is that *"the kingdom of God."* (Mark 10:13) is something to be entered. That is, we all start on the outside and need to enter. Jesus has made this point in one way or another several times and we have already covered it before. There are people inside *"the kingdom of God."* (Mark 10:15) There are people outside *"the kingdom of God."* (Mark 10:15) The choice people make on the outside of *"the kingdom of God."* (Mark 10:15) determines the entrance to living on the inside of *"the kingdom of God."* (Mark 10:15) This is not something where one goes in and out depending on their behavior. So many people believe that if they live the right way they will make the cut. There is a cut to be made. You can know for sure which side of the gate you are on. Everything in Mark's Gospel points consistently to a decision time and response of repentance and belief in the good news. This isn't some superficial event where without real meaning someone fills in a card, says a particular prayer, walks down an aisle, climbs up some stairs, goes through a ritual or signs a piece of paper. It certainly isn't something that someone else can do on your behalf. Being born into a particular family or culture and having some ritual performed on you as a baby might seem nice, but you will never find

Jesus advocating it. It may be a sincere act but Jesus didn't recommend it. Go ahead look for it. It simply isn't in there.

What Jesus is advocating here is an attitude that parallels a collection of attitudes normally seen in any young child. Without having a correct attitude you will never enter the kingdom of God.

Notice the word *"never."* (Mark 10:15) This isn't about something you can get into and then slip out of because you don't perform properly. Never means never. At one point in Jesus' life, as recorded in the Gospel of Matthew, Jesus promised that there will be people who will get to the gate of heaven and will be shocked to hear him say, *"I never knew you. Away from me, you evildoers!"* (Matthew 7:21-23) They will pull out their résumés and show him what they think is an impressive list of supporting reasons why his evaluation is incorrect. It will be too late. Their boat simply won't float.

So what do you think Jesus meant when he said, *"Like a little child"*? (Mark 10:15) Neither Jesus nor Mark explains that for us. We are left to figure it out on our own. And probably there are several characteristics to look at.

It seems to me that a primary characteristic of a little child is his readiness to trust those in authority. That is what we find so disgusting about child abusers. They first of all abuse the trust relationship that develops between the child and the adult. Once that bond is firmly cemented they move on to messing with the child's mind and conscience before they ever lay a hand on the child.

Those who have in some way been abused often find it extremely difficult to regenerate trust. But without a complete abandonment and an absolute trust in Jesus, no individual will ever enter the kingdom of God. That was true for me. It was true for my children. It is true for my grandchildren. It will be true for all succeeding generations. Trust. Trust in Jesus alone as the only solution for sin and as the only point of entry to a complete life on earth with the added benefit of a life with him in eternity.

If you are confused about how to enter this new form of life it may be that you are making this far too difficult. See ball. Hit ball.

Let's make it simple.

Are you convinced that Jesus is the only solution? Yes or no?

Do you understand he expects a 100% commitment? Yes or no?

Are you ready to make that commitment with all of the follow-through that comes along? Yes or no?

Are you going to make a decision right now? Yes or no?

Four yeses. One decision. Tell God and someone else if you just made it. If you have no one to tell, contact me and I will get back to you to help you with your next steps.

You don't have to have all your questions answered. You just have to put your complete trust in Jesus. If you find yourself saying, "I will trust him with everything but _____" I am glad you have identified your problem. But it won't do you any good whatsoever to try and handwrite a clause into the contract. Jesus simply won't initial it. You must get to the place where you will trust him with that part as well.

You really need to address the question of whether or not you will let your pet issue keep you from a full life in time and a spectacular life in eternity. After you decide to trust Jesus alone and start on your journey with him you will wonder how you ever thought your old grey, boring life was so much fun. Everything he asks you to give up is chump change.

Sometimes when people make that decision they get an overwhelming sense of relief. Here are some words written by my father telling the story of the moment he put his faith in Jesus alone. He had been an altar boy and by all reports a good kid. But he had not yet trusted Jesus. Of course, I don't know

Kid's Stuff

everything that transpired in the intervening years. But I do know he never looked back. I know that I was there by his bedside when he passed into the next life and met Jesus face to face. It was a holy peaceful time of grief for those of us who were left. As he was breathing his last my mother looked me in the eye and patted him on the shoulder and said, "He fought the good fight." That is a quote from the apostle Paul as he was facing his own graduation. (I Timothy 4:7)

Here, in his own words is my father's story of how he met Jesus in the city of Toronto. My father lived from 1903-1982. He wrote this account almost at the end of his life. He refers to Paul Rader who was a world class mass evangelist of the day.

> "It was in 1915 in a musty basement room of an old abandoned church at the north west corner of Yonge Street and Davenport Road, that I responded to a very earnest lay preacher's invitation to accept Jesus as my Saviour. Although I was serious and thought that I understood the way of salvation and had prayer together with my counsellor, I did not have peace in my heart and felt that I was not really converted.
>
> Two years later my chum and I both responded to an appeal given by Paul Rader at the conclusion of one of his brilliant messages, in a gospel campaign in Massey Hall.
>
> We both went down from the back of the top gallery for we both had been standing all evening (all seats full) to the front and shook Paul Rader's hand. Then we went to the enquiry room in the basement. I was counselled by a very godly retired missionary from China, a Mr. Douglas by name. He lived at 81 Victoria Avenue. I really can't understand why or how I remember his name and address. I was afraid someone from school might come in and see me. I was ashamed of myself and wanted to get out as fast as possible. I agreed with everything that Mr. Douglas had to say to me. After prayer together I scooted out. I still was not saved.

I was under deep conviction for over a year. I tried reading my Bible. I tried going to various churches where I thought I might learn the proper way to salvation all seemingly to no avail. I was desperate. Oh why was I born? I wished that I hadn't been, then I wouldn't have to seek an answer to where I will spend eternity. Satan certainly had my eyes blinded.

In 1918 I attended another Paul Rader campaign. I attended every night. Crowds were being saved each night, but not me—anxious as I was, I just could not grasp it. On the last night Rader pleaded with Christians to tell others four things: we are all sinners, the wages of sin is death, Christ died to pay the wages for all who believe, believe in Him. I believed! Hallelujah I knew I was saved. A burden rolled off my shoulders. No one counselled me or knew of this miracle, at the time. It was the closing moments of the campaign.

I walked 2 ¼ miles to home that night inwardly shouting, "Glory! Hallelujah! Jesus! Jesus! Jesus! Thank You! Thank you! Thank You!" My what an unexplainable joy was in my heart.

I have been trusting in the finished work of Jesus dying on the cross and rising again for my justification now for 64 years. Praise the Lord I have never once doubted my salvation and certainly have never regretted it, or found Him unfaithful. May he forgive my unworthiness and unfaithfulness. Ephesians 2:8-9. Look it up. Praise God. Syd Carter."

That was my father's heritage he passed on to me. No, he wasn't perfect. But he was committed. That testimony is not just a bunch of words. It sets the framework for everything I know about my father. He made his choice as a teenager. He lived it out. It doesn't bother me that I only remember him coming to one of my little league games. There was no question he loved me and wanted the best for me. We talked a lot. But I don't recall playing together very much. I do remember him bringing home to me many lessons from the Bible. He was very clever. But he was only self-educated. I recall that after he died, for several years I felt the impulse to ask him a question. But he was gone.

Dad wanted the very best for me and he gave me the best. My father took me to see Jesus as a very young boy. I am not referring to a picture that I saw. I don't mean a physical meeting. But the meeting was real. He showed me the history of Jesus and taught me to follow him and what he said. It was simple then. It's still simple. I put my complete trust in Jesus and I am so glad I did. It was and is the most important kid's stuff the world has ever known.

"Why do you call me good? No one is good—except God alone."

*Jesus
quoted in Mark 10:18*

16

Sad Stories

Why is it? We seem to like sad stories. At least those who tell them must think so. Heartbreak of some sort is a major theme in everything from movies to novels to country music songs.

I get a kick out of the words to country music songs. I don't particularly admit to enjoying the music except on occasion when I am feeling a little strange, bored or tired and driving in the car. But it is the words. They come up with so many interesting ways to tell a story of desertion or betrayal. Upbeat music. Downbeat story. Usually the story has something to do with somebody leaving somebody for somebody else. Somebody should figure out why we like that sort of thing. For sure, nobody likes it when it happens to them.

True tragic stories can break your heart.

I think one of the saddest stories I have ever heard—perhaps the saddest—is a true story from the life of Jesus.

Mark starts the story this way. *"As Jesus started on his way, a man ran up to him and fell on his knees before him. 'Good teacher,' he asked, "what must I do to inherit eternal life?"* (Mark 10:17)

There are some interesting things happening in the story even as it opens. Notice the intensity and devotion of this man. He ran to Jesus. He knelt before Jesus. He got right to it. He asked the correct question.

Look at that question. Preamble: "Good teacher." Question: "What must I do to inherit eternal life?" Now that is different. He presumed there was some activity for him to do or he wouldn't make it. He saw the end result of his desire as something to inherit. And he identified that desire as "eternal life." We haven't used that one in this book yet. Isn't that an interesting phrase? But I want you to bear in mind that is not a question out of Jesus' mouth so we can't be sure the concepts are all flowing in the direction of truth. I want to make a side point here. As you travel the road of life you will hear many things that sound reasonable; they might even sound Christian. But you can't be sure a message is correct just because the audience smiles and nods approval. The crowd can be very wrong. I don't want you to be a cynic and I don't want you to get hung up on vocabulary. I want you to be very careful with concepts. There might be many ways to convey a true concept using different words but you want to make sure you aren't buying into the concept just because the words tickle your ears. You want the truth, the whole truth and nothing but the truth so help you God.

So there is the question. I think this man is in the right zip code with that. What do you think? Now don't cheat—take a guess at how Jesus responds to it.

Option #1: Jesus gives him the straight, "Repent and believe the Good News" answer.

Option #2: Jesus takes a moment to commend him on his demeanor and respect before he goes into the, "Repent and believe the Good News" message.

Option #3: Jesus suggests he take it up with someone else.

Which one would you pick? Trick question. The answer is Option #4: None of the above.

In fact, you might think Jesus is borderline rude the way he answers this man. Folklore has created a version of Jesus that is not matched by reality. That commonly held version has a bland gentle softie who never got in anyone's face. This terrible myth has Jesus accepting everyone no matter what. The facts of the Bible tell a far different story. Jesus could be very confrontational when it was important. Here is a case where Jesus asks one of those probing questions that on the surface might appear to be combative. But his intention is not to pick a fight. Jesus wants this man to get a reality fix. It was true with this nice guy as it is with all of us. We have to understand our present coordinates on the road of life or we will never choose the correct direction. Now, let's get back to the conversation.

Jesus starts off by exploring the preamble. *"Why do you call me good?'* Jesus answered. *'No one is good—except God alone.'"* (Mark 10:18)

What do you think Jesus was getting at? Is there any other conclusion than surmising Jesus was trying to get his attention at an even deeper level and bring the man to realize that he in fact was talking to God himself? The other possibility is that the man was way over the top on the respect part and Jesus was refusing to accept that sort of veneration. But then, Jesus goes on to act like he is in fact God and has the authority to supply a definitive answer for him.

The rest of Jesus' answer is intriguing. Jesus is working up to exposing this man's point of vulnerability. He gives him a stock answer. *"You know the commandments: 'Do not murder, do not commit adultery, do not steal, do not give false testimony, do not defraud, honor your father and mother.'"* (Mark 10:19) He didn't hit all ten commandments but you get the idea. You do realize that all sin is in some way an extension of the ten biggies. He is pointing out to the man that he has a sin problem that must be dealt with. As far as the man has progressed on his spiritual journey he at least got to the point that unless something changed in his life his inheritance did not yet include eternal life. If one could gain eternal life by keeping this list with perfection and if this man already knew the list and had abided by it then all he needed from Jesus was a quick check up and, assuming he passes a quick and reassuring, "Well then, you should be good to go."

The man did respond with, *"'Teacher,' he declared, 'all these I have kept since I was a boy.'"* (Mark 10:20) I wonder why he dropped the "Good" this time. Maybe that was a touch point he hadn't yet resolved. That is just a guess. But I don't need to guess at the next part. He may have been one clean and slick camper but really, all of those commandments and all of the time? Not a chance. I am sure there is either some prevarication of the truth going on here or this man needs some serious self-awareness training. In either case, Jesus just blows on by his answer. Sometimes it just makes sense to let people hold on to some nonsense in favor of getting to the real issue.

If you think Jesus is being harsh here, think again. Whenever one is confronted with the truth there is a danger that they will take it as harshness and a lack of love. But Mark wanted us to understand the reality. *"Jesus looked at him and loved him."* (Mark 10:21) Isn't that something simple and special at the same time? Jesus paid attention to him; he looked him in the eye; he loved him. But he didn't lower the standard. He said, *"One thing you lack ..."* (We are coming back to that statement so put a bookmark on that thought.) *"... Go, sell everything that you have, and give to the poor and you will have treasure in heaven. Then come follow me."* (Mark 10:21) There we get a strong linkage between the man's desire for "eternal life" and Jesus' wording *"treasure in heaven."* (Mark 10:21) So we got that one out of the way. How good is that? Eternal life. Treasures in heaven. Kingdom of God. Did you read this question before? *"What can a man give in exchange for his soul?"* (Mark 8:37) If all this is real and true and not just a matter of overstated or symbolic semantics then it doesn't get any more serious than this. I can't imagine why anyone would read this and not have their eyes popping out if they have never heard all this before.

We have to get this amazing behavior Jesus demanded wrestled into place. What on earth is he getting at here? What do you think Jesus meant when he said, *"Go, sell everything that you have and give to the poor"*? (Mark 10:21) In this case, I think he meant that in order to gain eternal life this man needed to go sell everything and give to the poor. That is what I think. But why? I believe it is because money was his filing cabinet under which he organized the rest of the sins he wasn't about to acknowledge. He had built his road map around money. And his road map was taking him south. If he wanted to go north he needed to get with the program and have a major turn around. Does that make sense? In a word, he needed to repent. Notice the order. Repent, then follow. See ball. Hit ball.

And now for the saddest part. He is so close. So very close. But Jesus fingered his *"one thing."* (Mark 10:21) Mark tells us the awful truth. *"At this the man's face fell. He went away sad, because he had great wealth."* (Mark 10:22) Go figure. He got no eternal life—what he came for. He got sad—what he didn't come for. But he got the truth. And I expect he got sad for the rest of his natural life and much worse when he died. How could you go back to playing with your money and be happy about it if you knew it was the one thing that was going to keep you out of heaven? Oh and by the way, that was *"treasure in heaven"* (Mark 10:21) as well.

Back to the *"one thing"* (Mark 10:21) issue. At one point (not recorded by Mark) Jesus said, *"You cannot serve both God and Money."* (Matthew 6:24) The crazy thing is that people without much money keep serving money. They serve it in their imagination. They do the drive bys. They settle for the purchase of a new giant toy. It is always about the money. People have a wonderful way of masking their love of money. But you can't serve God and money at the same time. Don't you dare let money keep you out of heaven! There is nothing wrong with money. There is something terribly wrong with serving money. It just mocks you. You think, if I had some, I would be happy. Then you get some and you think, if I had some more I would be happy. So you go get some more. And guess what? Comfortable as the softest cushions in the world. Temporary glee. Not happy. Not soul satisfied. And even if the money could make you happy it wouldn't get you anything for the next life. The next life is longer. Pick the big issue. Eternity is in the balance. As far as planet earth is concerned a rich person is only a poor person with money. But as far as heaven is concerned, poor or rich on earth isn't a measurement that matters. So if your *"one thing"* is money, you had better think again.

Some people find that hard to do. Think again. Yes it is hard to accept that you have been building a castle in the sand and nothing permanent when the tide comes in. Yes it is hard to accept that your belief in family, religion, job, retirement, education, house, car, blah, blah, or whatever is not going to supply the fulfillment you long for. Until you come to the place where you get the concept of *"repent and believe"* firmly fixed in your soul you will be playing a game in which there are no winners. It is a cruel joke. Life as you know it is a riddle to which there is no solution. You want a solution. Jesus says he is it. Was he wrong?

What is the one thing you know you would have to give up in order to follow Jesus? What is the one thing you want the most out of life? If you had that one thing what would it get you? Keep digging. If you got that one thing the first thing supplied what would that get you? You should stay on that track until you get to the bottom of what you really want out of life. You will probably know when you hit pay dirt because you will well up with emotion. Actually, the one thing you want might be something noble and good. It could be something people say is an inalienable right of every person. And it could be that Jesus himself wants you to have it. But are you willing to give it up? Are you willing to put that one thing in the hands of Jesus and let him manage it? Are you willing to give him all the keys to the secret places of your heart and not keep a spare set hidden away somewhere?

When you get to the place where you can say, "It's all yours Jesus—my checkered past both good and bad—I give it to you along with the accumulated memories. It's all yours Jesus—my so called life as it is right now. It's all yours Jesus—all my future days for time and into eternity. I want you to take it all from this very moment on and do what you will with me."

The funny part to me—funny bewildering not funny ha ha—is that when you make that ultimate decision the curtains open and the real drama begins! It is like going from a black and white movie to a giant screen full brilliant color mega-screen. Honest. I know if you haven't experienced it you can't believe that yet. But it is the truth. The most stimulating, exciting, fulfilling and purposeful life on the planet is in following Jesus. Living goes from barely existing to inner joy that is so magnificent you can hardly stand it. Well. Not every day and every hour. But so often you won't be able to even imagine why your old toys were so important to you. You won't need them any more.

That's the deal. Nothing less will do. You don't want to be another tragic sad story do you?

"You are not far from the kingdom of God."

*Jesus
quoted in Mark 12:34*

17

The Rules

We started this book with baseball. At the risk of alienating the non-baseball people let's finish there. It is now October. Baseball fans know what that means. The real season is just beginning—the post season.

Over the years baseball has stayed the same but it has also changed. I am old enough to remember when they brought in a major change called the "designated hitter." I still can't get my head around that one after a generation. It seems so artificial and only half of baseball uses the concept. (If you don't know baseball, just forget it. It is too complicated.) Then they went and introduced inter-league play. I guess I am a traditionalist. I still can't get used to it.

I just don't like it when someone changes the rules in the middle of the game. But I guess those illustrations are about changing the game in the middle of the life. And I don't like changing the game in the middle of the life either.

But that is what we all must do according to Jesus. It is not so much that the rules have been changed as it is that they have been clarified.

Jesus is the clarifier.

"One of the teachers of the law came and heard them debating. Noticing that Jesus had given them a good answer he asked him, 'Of all the commandments, which is the most important?' 'The most important one,' answered Jesus, 'is this: 'Hear, O Israel, the Lord our God, the Lord is one. Love the Lord your God with all your heart and with all your soul and

with all your mind and with all your strength. The second is this: 'Love your neighbor as yourself.' There is no commandment greater than these." (Mark 12:29-31)

That makes it really straightforward. Relate properly to God. Relate properly to people. Done. We don't need to know anything else. We just need to act on it.

"Do do do do do. All you need is love. Do do do do do …" The Beatles get the credit. But they were a bunch of plagiarizers. And what is worse they left out the most important part. Love for God is the first part and it is the only seedbed out of which true love for humankind can grow.

But our story goes on.

"'Well said, teacher,' the man replied. 'You are right in saying that God is one and there is no other but him. To love him with all your heart, with all your understanding and with all your strength, and to love your neighbor as yourself is more important than all burnt offerings and sacrifices.'" (Mark 12:32-33)

Jesus liked his response but we will get to that in a moment.

I like the part here about these two rules being more important than all burnt offerings and sacrifices. Moses, under God, had introduced a system of animal sacrifices a long time ago. The tradition had stayed the same for loyal Hebrews down into Jesus' day. In fact, the occupying Roman government under King Herod had facilitated their observance of these religious rituals. Herod built a temple in Jerusalem that was magnificent. He actually extended the flat plateau on the top of the mountain so that he could make the area bigger and more spectacular. To do this he built retaining walls that would rival the size and stability of any built anywhere in history. Herod's temple was magnificent and brand spanking new in Jesus' day. The Hebrews were very proud of their system. It meant the world to them. The memory of happy feast times marked the passing of years. The sights, the sounds, the smells were all perfect. And there was the smell of the giant barbecue on which there was a constant supply of fresh meat given in sacrifice and then consumed as part of the family ritual. This was all so special. However, this teacher of the law—an ardent supporter and defender of the sacrificial system—was willing to put his religion in its place. He cared more about his relationships. I am so anxious for you to get that point. He realized that true meaning in life came not from his religion but from right relationships. No amount of preservation of religion is worth a thing compared to being right with God and then having the chance to get right with people.

Throughout this book I have resisted the word "church." I love the church. But just as Jesus minimized the use of the name "Christ" because it carried too much baggage for some, I have resisted the word "church" because many have had negative experiences connected with church. I don't want to confuse the issue. When I refer to the "church" I know it is fundamentally the very best facilitator of relationships with people and with God. I know that the church properly conceived is the best idea in town. I know that it has proven itself as being the most important organism on the face of the planet for societal change.

I know that Jesus said, *"I will build my church and the gates of Hades will not overcome it!"* (Matthew 16:18) Jesus was into church like you wouldn't believe. He knew that his plan for the ages depended on his followers building churches around the globe. Sigh—do I have to explain again—not buildings where people meet but groups of people who have to meet somewhere. And because they are committed to meeting they are willing to put up specialized buildings in which to do it. But it isn't ever useful to have a building that robs the people of the truth on which the church is built.

This leader who confronted Jesus with a good question about what comes first in the hierarchy of commandments was comforted by the fact that Jesus was advocating getting things in the right order.

And now to Jesus' response to this teacher of the law. It is at one and the same time hopeful and chilling.

"You are not far from the kingdom of God." (Mark 12:34)

Not there yet.

He knew the rules. He hadn't applied them properly by putting his faith and trust in Jesus alone for his solution.

Not there yet.

He knew the important place of love for God and love for neighbors. He probably was as fine a man as anyone in the vicinity. He was probably known for his upstanding morals and his care for people.

Not there yet.

He knew the issues. He hadn't come to the place of repentance and belief in the Good News so that he too could possess the kingdom of God.

Not there yet.

He was integrating a lot of elements. He was able to put his great religion in its proper perspective. But he had not yet submitted himself to the one who in the end is called in the Bible "Lord of lords, and King of kings." (Revelation 17:14)

Not there yet.

And you? Not there yet? I am fond of asking this question of my friends who are not there yet, "What is the worst thing that can happen if you give your life to Christ?" I have never heard an answer to that question that made true sense to me. I never found an answer that made me say, "Oh well then, this is not a good option for you!"

Not there yet?

"I am not sure this message is the truth, the whole truth and nothing but the truth."

Not there yet?

"I am afraid of all the changes that I will have to make."

Not there yet?

"I just don't know that I want to give up control of running my own life."

Not there yet?

"I guess I still want to try my own plan for a while and see if things get better."

Not there yet?

"I have too much invested in my present path to change now. The people around me would be shocked and I would be humiliated."

It is all so simple.

Jesus said, *"Save your life and you will lose it. Lose your life for me and for the gospel and you will save it."* (Mark 8:35)

Isn't it just like baseball? See ball. Hit ball.

But for your own sake—or as people are fond of saying for God's sake—won't you decide to get your eye on the ball? Now.

For those who say, "Yes! But how do I do that?" here is the path. Read Mark from top to bottom and assimilate its message. Then move on to John.

Read it and grasp another honest historical perspective on Jesus. Get to know him. Commit yourself to following him. Tell him. (You know the word "prayer." Prayer is just talking to God, so tell him.) Tell someone who will understand and help you. Tell me if you can't find someone; I will help you. Find a group of people who are resolute about following Jesus. Join them and work with them. They will walk with you through the rest of the process. You simply will not make it on your own. You need a new set of human relationships to develop with other followers of Jesus. How hard is that? Not very. Start today and prove to yourself that you are serious. Don't know where to start? Pick up the phone and call the person who would be most overjoyed by your response. That is probably the person who put this book in your hands. But if you honestly don't know where to turn, call me at 905-601-2110 or send me a brief e-mail at my BlackBerry gvc@kainos.org and I will get back to you—usually within a day. I love to hear from people who are just beginning their journey with Jesus. It is just that, for most I can't be there as often as you need, so we need to get you hooked up with a friend close by.

When we started our time together in this book I asked you to make a commitment. You can review it on page 15. Did you make that commitment then? And are you going to follow up on it now? It is my prayer that you will do just that.

Here are some questions for you to ponder.

1. Do these words of Jesus make sense to me?

2. As far as I can see, did this book (Hot Brass Tacks) fairly portray the words of Jesus?

3. Do these words of Jesus stir me? If so, does that scare me? Could these dozen statements change my world?

4. Do I find myself resisting this message? Why?

5. Have I clearly identified the list of things I am willing to give in exchange for my soul?

6. Have I thought through the price of rejecting Jesus and his message?

7. Am I willing to pay that price?

8. Have I done my research and observed others who follow Jesus in one of their get togethers and figured out if something positive is in the room? Or do I hold a negative opinion based on faded memories or an ineffective group?

9. Does that attractiveness appear to be based on love?

10. Am I ready to pick up the phone right now and take the next step?

Bible Reference Index

Matthew

Matthew 3:2	94
Matthew 4:17	74
Matthew 6:24	119
Matthew 7:21-23	109
Matthew 16:18	125

Mark

Mark 1:5	94
Mark 1:14	35
Mark 1:15	18, 20, 21, 22, 34, 35, 37, 42, 43, 44, 58, 66, 67, 70, 71, 73, 74, 75, 76, 88, 95
Mark 1:17	48, 49
Mark 1:27	24
Mark 2:5	59
Mark 2:7	59
Mark 2:9-11	59
Mark 2:17	58
Mark 3:13-15	80
Mark 4:1-20	63
Mark 4:3	71
Mark 4:12	63
Mark 4:15	64
Mark 4:16-17	65
Mark 4:18-19	65
Mark 4:20	67
Mark 4:26-29	71
Mark 4:28	66
Mark 4:30-34	73
Mark 4:33-34	71
Mark 4:4	64
Mark 4:5-6	65
Mark 4:7	65
Mark 4:8	66
Mark 4:9	63
Mark 6:8	81
Mark 7:14-15	86
Mark 7:18-23	87
Mark 7:27	92

Bible Reference Index

Mark 8:28	95
Mark 8:29	96
Mark 8:31	102
Mark 8:34	100, 102, 103
Mark 8:34-38	100
Mark 8:35	127
Mark 8:36	104
Mark 8:37	93, 118
Mark 8:38	104
Mark 10:13	108
Mark 10:13-15	108
Mark 10:15	108, 109
Mark 10:17	115
Mark 10:18	117
Mark 10:19	117
Mark 10:20	118
Mark 10:21	118, 119
Mark 10:22	119
Mark 10:45	102
Mark 12:29-31	124
Mark 12:32-33	124
Mark 12:34	126

Luke

Luke 9:23	101
Luke 10:29	12

John

John 1:1-17	86
John 1:3	85
John 1:14	36
John 1:29	102
John 1:29-31	95
John 8:32	28
John 10:35	50
John 13:35	75

Ephesians

Ephesians 2:8-9	112

www.ingramcontent.com/pod-product-compliance
Lightning Source LLC
Chambersburg PA
CBHW070503100426
42743CB00010B/1736